MANAGEMENT AND LEADERSHIP IN
EDUCATION

Series Editors: PETER RIBBINS AND JOHN SAYER

Managing to Motivate

Managing to Motivate:
A Guide for School Leaders

LINDA EVANS

CASSELL

London and New York

Cassell

Wellington House
125 Strand
London WC2R 0BB

370 Lexington Avenue
New York
NY 10017-6550

First published 1999

British Library Cataloguing-in-Publication Data
A catalogue record for this book is available from the British Library.

ISBN 0-304-70617-5

Typeset by York House Typographic Ltd, London
Printed and bound in Great Britain by
Biddles Ltd, Guildford and King's Lynn.

Contents

Introduction

In the UK the teaching profession is poised, at the beginning of the twenty-first century, on the brink of change. In the 1998 Green Paper (DfEE, 1998) the Government presented its 'new vision of the teaching profession', reflecting its concern to raise standards in education. The bywords are 'modernization of the profession', 'a new professionalism' and 'a first class profession'. There is reference to 'performance management', 'a career of learning', and to rewarding 'excellent teaching'. Clearly, this government wants to get the best out of its teachers.

But getting the best out of teachers is not a simple and straightforward issue. It is not just a question of paying them enough, or improving conditions of service, or offering financial incentives to excel, or raising the profession's status. Of course, some of these things will certainly help but, on their own, they are inadequate. Getting the best – the *very* best – out of teachers is something over which governments do not have much direct control. It occurs much closer to home. If it is to happen at all, getting the best out of teachers will occur in the schools and colleges in which they work – and it will be achieved by good leadership. It will be achieved by headteachers – and other people in leadership positions – motivating teachers to give of their best. This is clearly recognized by one secondary headteacher, who begins his booklet, *366 Pieces of Advice for the Secondary Headteacher*:

> All good schools have good staff and a Head can do little on his own – possibly the most important aspect of the job is motivating and developing the staff of the school.

> 1. *Motivating staff* is essential – you should have analysed how you are trying to do it, have a policy for it and be evaluating how successful you are. (Stephens, 1998a, p. 1)

The importance of leadership is now recognized by the British Government. It is highlighted as a key issue in the 1998 Green Paper (DfEE, 1998) and it is reflected in the introduction of national standards for headteachers (Teacher Training Agency (TTA), 1998) and of mandatory headship training. In particular, the importance of *motivational* leadership is acknowledged within the national standards for headteachers (TTA, 1998, p. 11):

> Headteachers lead, motivate, support, challenge and develop staff to secure improvement ... They:
> ... iv. motivate and enable all staff in their school to carry out their respective roles to the highest standard ...
> ... vii. sustain their own motivation and that of other staff ...

The crucial role of headteachers and principals in influencing what teachers do – and which has long been recognized by educational researchers who work in this field – is summed up by Lortie (1975, p. 197):

> The principal's decisions can vitally affect the teacher's working conditions. He assigns teachers to classes and students to particular teachers; the actual work may be done by assistants, but the principal remains the court of final appeal. The principal is the ultimate authority on student discipline, and parents turn to him for redress when they think their children have been improperly treated. The allocation of materials, space, and equipment is handled through the principal's office, and time schedules are worked out under his supervision. His decisions can, in short, affect the teacher's work duties for months at a time.

Like Tony Stephens, the headteacher whom I quote above, I believe that motivating staff is one of a headteacher's or principal's most important roles. My belief is not based on a vague impression or an idea that I have plucked out of the air. It is based on research evidence that reveals teacher morale, job satisfaction and motivation to be influenced much more by school management and leadership than by any other factor. It is based on research evidence that school leaders can – and do – have a major impact on how teachers feel about, and how they do, their jobs.

But it is one thing for you, as a school leader, to realize that you play a key role in influencing teacher morale, job satisfaction and motivation, and another to know *how* you influence them – how to go about the business of getting the best out of teachers. This book explains how. It presents research evidence of what motivates teachers – and what demotivates them – and offers guidelines for approaches to school leadership that manages to motivate.

I emphasize that this book has been written as a guide for *any* school leader (and those who aspire to leadership roles) – not just headteachers – and not just in the UK. The principles underpinning motivational leadership are precisely the same for any leadership role. Whether you work in the pre-school, primary/elementary, or secondary sector of education (or even if you work in post-compulsory education), if you hold responsibility for managing the behaviour of other teachers – whether it be as a headteacher or principal, head of a faculty or department, team leader, deputy head or assistant principal, or whatever – you are what I categorize as a school leader, and this book was written with you in mind.

In writing the book I drew on the work of educational researchers who have made key contributions to the study of teachers' working lives, but the main research basis is my own study of teacher morale, job satisfaction and motivation. I provide outline details of this study in the Appendix. This study sought teachers' views on factors affecting their attitudes to their work. Twenty teachers were interviewed, some on two separate occasions with at least one year's gap between the interviews. I did not seek headteachers' views since they were irrelevant to what I was investigating. This was not a study of school management, but it did, nevertheless, reveal teachers' perceptions of leadership and management. It was perceptions – not objective reality – that I wanted to discover, since it is these (even if they are *mis*perceptions) that influence morale, job satisfaction and motivation. This book therefore represents a much-neglected aspect of the study of school management and leadership – the perspective of 'the managed' or 'the led'. After all, if we want to get the best out of teachers we need to listen to what *they* have to say.

CHAPTER 1

What makes teachers tick? What makes teachers cross? Understanding morale, job satisfaction and motivation

Introduction

If school leaders and managers are to get the best out of the teachers whom they lead and manage they need to understand what makes teachers tick. They need to appreciate what kinds of things enthuse and challenge teachers; what gives them a 'buzz'; what interests and preoccupies them; what has them walking six inches off the ground; what sends them home happy and satisfied. They also need to know what irritates and angers teachers; what hurts and upsets them; what makes them dread going to work; what makes them desperate to change jobs; what frustrates and demoralizes them.

Getting the best out of staff consistently is not a matter of good luck. It does not occur incidentally and it is not automatic. It is a skill. Like all skills, it may be learned, practised and refined. Like all skills, it is easier to master if the principles and the laws that underpin it are recognized and understood. The skill of being able to get the best out of people is underpinned by laws of human nature: more specifically, of applied psychology. In the context of work, understanding human nature and what makes people behave as they do stems from an even narrower field of study within applied psychology: occupational psychology. The knowledge and understanding that are derived from applied psychology and, in particular, occupational psychology, underpin management theory. In turn, an understanding of management theory – and the application of this understanding to management behaviour – improves management skills.

If school managers and leaders are, therefore, to get the best out of teachers they need to understand what kinds of things raise or lower teachers' morale; what gives them job satisfaction or dissatisfaction; and what motivates or demotivates them.

Understanding morale, job satisfaction and motivation

Job satisfaction, morale and motivation are not simple and straight-forward to understand. They have been the foci of study from around the 1930s and much research into what they are, as concepts, as well as what influences them was carried out in the middle decades of the twentieth century. Research evidence, which has been the basis of management theory, challenges and contradicts the kind of commonsense reasoning and assumptions that attribute morale and satisfaction levels to factors such as pay and professional status. Below, I examine what research and scholarship in this field have revealed about these three attitudes – which is how, in occupational psychology terminology, they are known.

The concepts

Job satisfaction, morale and motivation are not obscure terms. They are frequently used in contexts that involve consideration of people at work. They are part of everyday, work-related vocabulary. Employers use the terms when discussing their workforces; managers use them when discussing their staff; news reporters use them when reporting announcements of pay freezes, pay rises, strikes and industrial disputes; the general public uses them when discussing such reports. Everybody seems to know what they mean. They do not appear to be ambiguous. There does not appear to be anything complex about them. But how many people could actually explain precisely what morale is, or what job satisfaction is, or what the difference between the two is?

There is, of course, no real need for most people to be able to define these job-related attitudes, nor to develop anything more than an understanding of them that is perfectly adequate for day-to-day use. For those who have made them the focus of serious academic study, though, morale, job satisfaction and motivation have been analysed as concepts, examined, discussed and defined. This has been invaluable in understanding these attitudes and what influences them, and those who wish to foster high morale, job satisfaction and motivation amongst staff will find the insight afforded by a greater understanding of the concepts helpful.

Morale

Morale is the concept that, of the three, seems to have been the most difficult to get to grips with. Within the research and academic community in particular, those who take conceptual analysis and definition seriously accept that morale is a very nebulous, ill-defined concept, whose meaning is generally inadequately explored. The concept was being examined at least as early as the 1950s, mainly in the USA. Guion (1958) refers to the 'definitional limb' on which writers about morale find themselves and indeed, as Smith (1976) points out, some writers avoid using the term in order to eliminate the problems of defining it. Williams and Lane (1975), employing a chameleon analogy, emphasize the elusiveness of the concept. Redefer (1959, p. 59) describes it as a 'complex and complicated area of investigation' and one which lacks a succinct definition, while Williams (1986, p. 2) writes that 'the attempts at defining and measuring morale in the literature seem like a quagmire', and, 40 years ago, Baehr and Renck (1959, p. 188) observed that 'literature on morale yields definitions which are as varied as they are numerous'.

One source of disagreement has been whether morale may be applied to individuals, or whether it relates only to groups. Many writers focus exclusively on group morale and employ definitions incorporating phrases such as 'shared purpose' (Smith, 1976), 'group goals' and 'feelings of togetherness' (Guba, 1958):

> Morale can be defined as a prevailing temper or spirit in the individuals forming a group. (Bohrer and Ebenrett, in Smith, c. 1988).

> ... a confident, resolute, willing, often self-sacrificing and courageous attitude of an individual to the function or tasks demanded or expected of him by a group of which he is part ... (McLaine, in Smith, c. 1988)

My own work in this field (see, for example, Evans, 1992; 1997a; 1998) has led me to interpret morale as primarily an attribute of the individual, which is determined in relation to individual goals. Individual goals may be explicit as, for example, a clear set of ambitions, but in many cases they are implicit in individuals' reactions to situations which arise and responses to choices offered. Group morale certainly exists, I believe, but it is merely the collectivization of the morale of the individuals who form the group. Guion (1958) appreciates the significance of individuals' goals in determining morale. His definition of morale, also adopted by Coughlan, is close to my own interpretation of the concept: 'Morale is the extent to which an individual's needs are satisfied and the extent to which the individual perceives that satisfaction as stemming from his total job situation' (Coughlan, 1970, pp. 221-2).

Yet this definition falls short, I feel, in that it fails to distinguish between morale and job satisfaction. Although they are often, in everyday parlance, used interchangeably, morale and job satisfaction are not the same thing. My interpretation of the distinction between them is that job satisfaction is present-oriented and morale is future-oriented. Both are states of mind, but I perceive satisfaction to be a *response* to a situation whereas morale is *anticipatory*. I interpret morale as a state of mind which is determined by reference to anticipated future events: by the anticipated form that they will take and their anticipated effect upon satisfaction. It is dependent upon, and guided by, past events in so far as past experiences provide a basis upon which to anticipate. The teacher who believes, for example, that the appointment of a new headteacher or principal to her school will improve the quality of her working life is manifesting high morale. The teacher who, on the other hand, is dissatisfied with his current headteacher is manifesting low job satisfaction. Thus high morale may exist alongside dissatisfaction. Evaluations of the present constitute job satisfaction-related issues, whereas anticipation of the future constitutes morale.

My definition of morale modifies that of Guion (1958) to accommodate my own interpretation of the concept: *Morale is a state of mind encompassing all of the feelings determined by the individual's anticipation of the extent of satisfaction of those needs which s/he perceives as significantly affecting his/her total (work) situation.*

Job satisfaction

Job satisfaction was the subject of much examination from the 1930s, and particularly so in the middle decades of the twentieth century. Locke (1969), for example, estimates that, as of 1955, over 2000 articles on the subject had been published and that, by 1969, the total may have exceeded 4000. Despite this, those whose research is in this area face problems arising from a general lack of conceptual clarity. There is no real consensus about what job satisfaction is, and relatively few definitions are available. Mumford describes it as 'a nebulous concept'. She writes:

> The literature on job satisfaction is of equally small help in providing us with an understanding of the concept. There appear to be no all-embracing theories of job satisfaction and work on the subject has been focused on certain factors thought to be related to feelings of satisfaction or dissatisfaction at work. Few studies take a wide and simultaneous survey of a large number of related variables. Job dissatisfaction has been found easier to identify and measure than job satisfaction. (Mumford, 1972, p. 4)

> Two points emerge clearly from the work that has been done up to date. One is the elusiveness of the concept of job satisfaction. What does it mean? ... The second is the complexity of the whole subject. (Mumford, 1972, p. 67)

Over 25 years after Mumford made these observations, there has been little change. Indeed, a general neglect of concern for conceptual clarity seems to have pervaded more recent work in this field, prompting Nias, in the course of her work on teachers' job satisfaction, to comment in 1989, 'I encountered several difficulties ... The first was a conceptual one. As a topic for enquiry, teachers' job satisfaction has been largely ignored. Partly in consequence, it lacks clarity of definition' (Nias, 1989, p. 83).

In order to appreciate the points that both Nias and Mumford make, and in order to attempt to uncover what job satisfaction is, it is worth comparing a few of the definitions and interpretations that are available.

Schaffer's (1953, p. 3) interpretation of job satisfaction is one of fulfilment of individuals' needs: 'Overall job satisfaction will vary directly with the extent to which those needs of an individual which can be satisfied in a job are actually satisfied; the stronger the need, the more closely will job satisfaction depend on its fulfilment'. Sergiovanni (1968) also supports the personal needs' fulfilment interpretation, whereas Lawler (1994, p. 99) focuses on expectations rather than needs: 'Overall job satisfaction is determined by the difference between all the things a person feels he should receive from his job and all the things he actually does receive'. Locke (1969), however, dismisses both needs and expectations in favour of values. He defines job satisfaction as 'the pleasurable emotional state resulting from the appraisal of one's job as achieving or facilitating the achievement of one's job values' (Locke, 1969, p. 316), whilst Nias (1989) accepts Lortie's (1975) interpretation of job satisfaction as a summary of the total rewards experienced (in teaching).

My own interpretation of job satisfaction goes beyond any other that I have found in the literature in this field. It is grounded in my research and was developed out of analysis of my findings. I identify two components of job satisfaction, which I refer to as *job fulfilment* and *job comfort*. My identification of these two components stems from my analysis of job satisfaction, which led me to the realization that the term 'satisfaction' is ambiguous. We can talk about customer satisfaction, for example, and about the satisfaction of conquering Everest. The two are quite distinct. The first concerns how satis*factory* something is, and the second concerns how satis*fying* it is. The problem in researching teachers' job satisfaction has been that, because of the general lack of conceptual clarity, there has been no agreement about what job satisfaction means and the ambiguity which I identify has been overlooked. Very few researchers have attempted to define job satisfaction: most have simply assumed that everyone understands the concept. They have tended simply to ask teachers, either through interviews or through questionnaires, about sources of job satisfaction and dissatisfaction, but confusion has arisen because teachers' interpretations of the concept differed.

Some have interpreted it as involving only those features of their work that are fulfilling, or satisfying, whereas others have applied a wider interpretation, incorporating both satisfying and satisfactory aspects of their work. What has resulted, therefore, is a distorted picture, yet this distortion and the confusion that underpins it seem to have gone unnoticed. My conceptualization, and my identification of two components – job comfort, which concerns how satisfactory something is, and job fulfilment, which concerns how satisfying something is – provide the clarification that is necessary if we are to build up an accurate picture of teachers' job satisfaction.

I define job satisfaction as *a state of mind encompassing all those feelings determined by the extent to which the individual perceives her/his job-related needs to be being met*, and, more narrowly, job fulfilment as *a state of mind encompassing all those feelings determined by the extent of the sense of personal achievement which the individual attributes to his/her performance of those components of his/her job which s/he values.*

Motivation

If definitions of morale and of job satisfaction are thin on the ground, those of motivation are even more of a rarity. This is quite surprising because, as a topic, motivation has been the focus of much study. The plethora of literature that began to emerge, principally from the United States, from the 1930s onwards, and which was aimed at informing the industrial world how it might best increase output and efficiency by improving workers' performance, has been the medium for the dissemination and critical analysis of several motivation theories.

It is certainly the case, as Steers *et al.* (1996, p. 9) point out, that 'the concept of motivation has received considerable attention over the course of this century', but this attention has, for the most part, focused on clarification of what motivation encompasses, and on identifying its features. This has resulted in descriptions or inter-pretations of motivation rather than definitions. Some of the major studies of motivation fail to incorporate conceptual definitions. Maslow (1954), for example, whose work *Motivation and Personality* is generally considered seminal, fails to provide an explicit definition of motivation. The outcome has been, without doubt, and with a few exceptions, the provision of valuable elucidation of what motivation may look like and how it may be recognized, but not of what, precisely, it is.

Steers *et al.* (1996, p. 8) suggest, 'What is needed is a description which sufficiently covers the various components and processes associated with how human behavior is activated'. They present what they describe as an illustrative selection of definitions of motivation,

although I categorize some of these as descriptions or interpretations
rather than definitions:

> ... the contemporary (immediate) influence on the direction, vigor and
> persistence of action. (Atkinson, 1964, cited in Steers *et al.*, 1996, p. 8)

> ... how behavior gets started, is energized, is sustained, is directed, is
> stopped, and what kind of subjective reaction is present in the organism
> while all this is going on. (Jones, 1955, cited in Steers *et al.*, 1996, p. 8)

> ... a process governing choice made by persons or lower organisms among
> alternative forms of voluntary activity. (Vroom, 1964, cited in Steers *et al.*,
> 1996, p. 8)

> ... motivation has to do with a set of independent/dependent variable
> relationships that explain the direction, amplitude, and persistence of an
> individual's behavior, holding constant the effects of aptitude, skill, and
> understanding of the task, and the constraints operating in the environ-
> ment. (Campbell and Pritchard, 1976, cited in Steers *et al.*, 1996, p. 8)

My own definition of motivation, which I apply to my research and
to the analyses throughout this book, is: *motivation is a condition, or the
creation of a condition, that encompasses all of those factors that determine
the degree of inclination towards engagement in an activity*. This incorporates recognition that motivation does not necessarily determine
whether or not activity occurs, it need only determine the extent to
which individuals feel inclined towards activity. It is, of course,
possible to be motivated to do something, without actually doing it.

In my references throughout this book to teachers' motivation I
also employ the terms 'motivator' and 'demotivator'. I define these:
a motivator is the impetus that creates inclination towards an activity, and *a
demotivator is the impetus for disinclination towards an activity*.

What influences morale, job satisfaction and motivation?

Ask anyone in the street how to raise teacher morale and, almost
certainly, s/he will suggest increasing pay. Ask what factors might
have recently created dissatisfaction amongst British teachers, and
the answers from those who read newspapers or watch the television
news will probably include references to discipline problems created
by unruly pupils, class sizes, lowered professional status, and changes
to pension regulations. In fact, in January 1997, *The Times Educational
Supplement* gave extensive coverage to teacher morale, motivation
and satisfaction in the UK, which began with publication of a survey
of teachers' attitudes that it had conducted in 1996, revealing, it was
reported, that 'Morale in Britain's staffrooms has hit rock bottom'
(Sutcliffe, 1997). This was attributed, in the main, to Government
reforms and conditions of service:

> Teachers are feeling disillusioned, demoralized and angry at being forced
> to carry out unpopular Government policies, while being constantly
> blamed for society's ills.
>
> They are fed up with having to teach children in ever larger classes,
> working in schools which are dilapidated, underfunded and overstretched.
> (Sutcliffe, 1997)

As well as focusing upon factors such as these, the media pro-
mulgates commonly-held assumptions that teachers' motivation is
pay-related. For example, in response to the report of the Interim
Advisory Committee on teachers' pay and conditions in 1991, it was
suggested in *The Times Educational Supplement* that, in relation first to
recruitment and, second, to improvement, pay could be a key motivator:

> If our teaching force is to be recruited from among the brightest and the
> best of our graduates, the money must come first. There is then every
> chance that quality will follow. But the graduate in question needs to be
> attracted by a competitive starting salary, and confident of a career progres-
> sion that will reward ability and application. (Anon., 1991)

Pay is also reported as an effective motivator in relation to improving job performance:

> This Government will one day have to pay its teaching force sufficiently
> highly to achieve the quality of education to which it has so far merely paid
> lip service. (Andain, 1990)

> Teachers work hard and standards are improving in some aspects of school
> work. But they are not good enough, nor are they improving fast enough,
> because teachers are not being paid for high-quality performance. (Tom-
> linson, 1990)

There is no shortage of evidence that pay is widely considered to be
an important factor in the retention of teachers. The allowances paid
to teachers in schools in designated Social Priority Areas, in accordance with the recommendations of the Plowden Report on primary
education (CACE, 1967), were intended to retain staff in these
schools. More recently, Blackbourne (1990) reported on a huge
turn-out of teachers at an alternative jobs fair: 'And who can blame
them? A spokesman for the Bacteriostatic Water Systems stall said two
of the company's top earners were ex-teachers with salaries per
month – not per year – of more than £25,000'.

Most recently of all, the UK Government has, in its 1998 Green
Paper, put forward specific ideas for the implementation of a
performance-related pay system for headteachers and classroom
teachers:

> Rewarding heads for good performance is appropriate in its own right. It is
> also central to the development of a school culture which encourages and

rewards excellence. Each year, heads and governing bodies should agree targets for school improvement against which the head's performance would be assessed and which should form the basis for decisions on performance-related pay. Pay enhancements should depend on clear evidence of progress in pupil attainment. (DfEE, 1998, para. 43)

We propose two pay ranges for classroom teachers, with a performance threshold giving access to a new, higher range for high performing teachers with a track record of consistently strong performance. (DfEE, 1998, para. 65)

We therefore propose a pay system with the following objectives:

• It should attract, retain and motivate all staff. (DfEE, 1998, para. 71)

Evidence that pay, conditions of service, status and other centrally-initiated factors influence motivation, morale and job satisfaction are, however, based on assumption rather than research. The complete picture is much more complex than commonsense reasoning and anecdotal evidence would lead us to believe. Let me make it clear at the outset that I accept that factors such as these referred to above do affect teachers' attitudes to their work, but research has revealed that they are not the main influences on morale, job satisfaction and motivation. In order to uncover precisely 'what makes teachers tick, and what makes teachers cross', it is necessary to examine the findings of some of this research.

One of the key studies in the field is that of Herzberg (1968). His research was not focused on teachers: it involved research into the job satisfaction of engineers and accountants in Pittsburgh. Nevertheless, although it is a contentious study which has been criticized on methodological grounds, it is generally regarded as seminal and it has certainly drawn considerable attention from other researchers in the occupational psychology field.

From analysis of his research findings Herzberg formulated a theory, which he calls his Motivation–Hygiene Theory, or, as it is also known, the Two Factor Theory. Herzberg's research findings revealed two distinct sets of factors – one set which motivates or satisfies employees, and one set which may demotivate or create dissatisfaction. This theory has been applied to, and tested in, education contexts (see, for example, Farrugia, 1986; Nias, 1981; Young and Davis, 1983). According to Herzberg there are five features of work which motivate people, or which are capable of providing job satisfaction. These are: achievement; recognition (for achievement); the work itself; responsibility; and advancement. Herzberg refers to these as motivation factors, and they all share the distinction of being factors that are intrinsic to the work. Those features that Herzberg identifies as capable of demotivating, or creating dissatisfaction, are labelled hygiene factors and are all extrinsic to the work. These are listed as: salary; supervision; interpersonal relations; policy and administration; and working conditions.

The essential point of Herzberg's theory is that hygiene factors are not capable of motivating or satisfying people, even though they may be sources of dissatisfaction. Removing hygiene factors that are creating dissatisfaction does not – indeed, *cannot* – create job satisfaction because hygiene factors are incapable of doing so. So, for example, if employees are dissatisfied with or demotivated by the salary that they receive, giving them a pay rise will not motivate or satisfy them. It will merely ensure that they are not *dis*satisfed with their pay. Herzberg, in fact, likens a pay rise to 'a shot in the arm', which may offer a temporary boost, but whose effects are short-lived. According to him, removing sources of dissatisfaction does not ensure job satisfaction: only the intrinsic factors – the five motivation factors – are able to do that:

> In summary, two essential findings were derived from this study. First, the factors involved in producing job satisfaction were separate and distinct from the factors that led to job dissatisfaction. Since separate factors needed to be considered, depending on whether job satisfaction or job dissatisfaction was involved, it followed that these two feelings were not the obverse of each other. Thus, the opposite of job satisfaction would not be job dissatisfaction, but rather *no* job satisfaction; similarly, the opposite of job dissatisfaction is *no* job dissatisfaction, not satisfaction with one's job. The fact that job satisfaction is made up of two unipolar traits is not unique, but it remains a difficult concept to grasp. (Herzberg, 1968, pp. 75-6)

Herzberg's hygiene factors are those which would generally influence how satisfactory a job is considered, whereas motivation factors relate more to the extent to which work is satisfying. There is no evidence that Herzberg acknowledges this. Indeed, his theory emphasizes what has often been regarded as a revelation: that the opposite of satisfaction is not dissatisfaction but 'no satisfaction', and that the opposite of dissatisfaction is not satisfaction, but 'no dissatisfaction'. The issue is, I believe, much more simple and straightforward. Since one category relates to factors which are capable only of making things satisfactory, and the other to factors which are capable of satisfying, then, clearly, they *are* distinct and separate. Indeed, they equate to what I have identified as job comfort and job fulfilment. But realization of this should not form the basis of a theory; it merely follows on from awareness that there are separate, but related, components of what has tended to be regarded as a single concept. What Herzberg presents as a theory is, in my view, nothing more than conceptual misunderstanding that arises out of failure to recognize the ambiguity of the key term.

While some writers evidently interpret job satisfaction as encompassing both what is satisfying and what is satisfactory, there are those whose interpretation of the term is apparently narrower and concerned only with what is satisfying. There is, in fact, evidence that Herzberg (1968) falls into this category, since his theory emphasizes that dissatisfaction is not the same as no satisfaction. This suggests that he considers 'dissatisfaction' to mean 'unsatisfactory', which does not fall within the parameters of what he relates to job satisfaction, and that he considers 'no satisfaction' to mean 'lacking the capacity to be satisfying'. However, it is only possible to make assumptions, since Herzberg fails to define either job satisfaction or motivation. In fact, not only does he fail to define them but he fails to distinguish between them and seems to use the two terms interchangeably. Again, I consider this to be a conceptual weakness that impoverishes his work. Motivation, as I have pointed out, is not the same as job satisfaction: I have defined each distinctly.

It is not only Herzberg's work which provides evidence that pay does not motivate. Although the UK Government proposes to introduce it for teachers, performance-related pay, or merit pay, has been revealed by research to be generally flawed. Johnson (1986) reveals the failure of a number of merit pay schemes introduced in the United States during the twentieth century and points out that some were even found to demotivate. Chandler's (1959) research in the United States compared morale levels in schools which used merit pay schemes and schools which did not. His findings revealed no significant difference between the two. Mathis' (1959) research findings corroborate this, and Mayston (1992) concluded that performance-related pay is an over-simplistic approach to tackling problems of teacher motivation, that its success is questionable, and that it even has the potential for demotivating.

Other research, whilst not focused specifically on evaluating merit pay, has demonstrated that professional motivation, morale and job satisfaction are not dependent upon pay:

> Differences in salary were not related to differences in career satisfaction. This is quite consistent with Lortie's observations that teaching as a career is relatively unstaged and front-loaded ... Individuals who persist in teaching recognize from the outset that financial rewards are limited. (Chapman, 1983, p. 48)

> We seem to be overly concerned with providing adequate salaries, benefits, facilities, and other 'pleasantries'. ... Yet these factors apparently have little potential to provide for adequate job satisfaction, for higher level need fulfilment. At best, these efforts protect teachers from dissatisfaction in work and ensure that teachers will continue to participate as 'good' organizational members.

> The really potent factors, the factors with motivational potential, the real
> determiners of job satisfaction, are harder to come by. (Sergiovanni, 1968,
> pp. 263-4)

My own research into factors influencing morale, job satisfaction
and motivation amongst teachers, carried out between 1988 and
1993 (see Appendix and, for full details of the research design, Evans
1998, pp. 46-56), revealed conditions of service, within which category I include salary, to have only limited influence on teachers'
attitudes to their work. The comments of one of my interviewees
reflect, in general, the attitudes of most of my sample:

> I haven't looked at my pay slip for the last 12 months ... and I don't know
> why – it's not a driving force any more. At one stage I used to long for pay
> day and look carefully at how much I'd got ... but it doesn't bother me any
> more.

However, this raises the issue of what it is – if it is not pay – that does
motivate teachers.

It is very difficult to draw out of the available literature accurate
evidence of what motivates teachers because, as I have already
pointed out, in many cases the distinction between motivation and
job satisfaction and morale is not clarified. Similar difficulties occur
over finding evidence of sources of teacher morale and job satisfaction. Moreover, I have already referred to the problem that arises,
when trying to make sense of the literature on job satisfaction, out of
not knowing, first, whether researchers interpret job satisfaction as
involving only fulfilment or whether they adopt a wider interpretation, and, second, which of these two interpretations was adopted by
the teachers upon whom the research was focused. Thus, for example, evidence presented in the literature that teachers find a pleasant
working environment and nice décor in the staffroom to be sources
of job satisfaction cannot be taken at face value – indeed, its mean-
ingfulness is limited unless those presenting the evidence also
present their definitions or interpretations of job satisfaction and
explain how they ascertained, in the process of carrying out their
research, what interpretations teachers held. Nevertheless, since it
serves as a broad indicator, it is worth considering some of the
evidence that purports to reveal factors that influence teachers'
attitudes. It is also worth examining, as a starting point, evidence of
how teachers feel about their work and what they report liking and
disliking about it.

There is much evidence to corroborate Herzberg's (1968) findings in respect of those factors which he identifies as motivation
factors: achievement, recognition (for achievement), responsibility,
advancement, and the work itself. In his classic study of American

teachers' working lives, Lortie (1975) categorizes factors such as these as psychic rewards and, as a category, psychic rewards were identified by his sample as the greatest source of job satisfaction. In particular, the reward of feeling that they had 'reached' students, and that students had learned, was identified as a source of satisfaction by the greatest number of Lortie's teachers.

Chapman's (1983) study, which focused on 437 American college graduates who had entered the teaching profession and were still teaching, revealed recognition and approval to be key motivational factors.

Kasten's (1984, p. 4) sample of American teachers referred to the 'delights and satisfaction of working with children', 'the importance of the job', 'personal rewards', 'variety in the work', and 'a feeling of competence'.

Farrugia (1986), Galloway et al. (1985) and Nias (1981; 1989) all make explicit reference to a broad consistency between their research findings and Herzberg's Two Factor Theory. More specifically, Nias (1989) refers to 'affective' and 'competence-related' rewards, both of which she relates to working with children. Other sources of satisfaction reported by her sample of 99 British graduate teachers include extension of personal skills and qualities – both through teaching and through other responsibilities – and feeling autonomous.

The importance of leadership and collegial support as motivators has been emphasized in many studies (see, for example, ILEA, 1986; Johnson, 1986; Nias, 1980; Nias et al., 1989). Where these factors are reported as sources of satisfaction or motivation, it is evidently the recognition and approbation which they provide for teachers that is important. Nias (1989, p. 146) provides comments from three of her teacher interviewees:

> The head's a tremendous force in the school ... she can be a real demon and sometimes the tension gets you down because you know she's watching you all the time, but you feel really pleased when she pats you on the back.

> The head says he's pleased with what I've done so far and that's given me confidence that I'm on the right track.

> We have a new head and she's made us all feel much better about things because she takes a real interest in what we're doing – comes round and has a look, talks to the children about their work, asks us before she buys equipment, all that sort of thing.

My own research into teachers' attitudes to their jobs revealed school-specific factors to be much more influential on levels of job satisfaction, morale and motivation than were externally-instigated and centrally-imposed factors. One of the key findings of my research was that job satisfaction, morale and motivation are predominantly contextually-determined. This is because it is the context of teachers' working lives that represents the realities of the job. Only one of my interviewees, Jane,[1] a mainscale teacher who had reached the top of the salary scale, was dissatisfied with teachers' pay. The same teacher also made reference to the wider issue of the demoralizing effect of teachers' low status in society. Only one other teacher, Kay, who held a promoted post – what was then an incentive allowance B – identified pay as a source of satisfaction. A few teachers even identified pay specifically as a relatively unimportant factor in relation to motivation. Issues such as the introduction of the national curriculum, the imposition of contractual hours and the five 'Baker days', designated for in-service training, were either relegated to subsidiary levels of importance in teachers' assessments of what affected their morale and/or job satisfaction, or were assessed within the context of their own school situations, and in relation to how these contexts shaped them. Pat, for example, spoke of how her school's management was a constraint on her doing her job, including her implementation of the national curriculum:

> You ask yourself, 'Why am I bothering? Why am I giving up time in the evenings . . . time in the holidays, to do work which is not directly related to the class, to find that . . . it's being ignored?' – or to find that you go to a management meeting with the head and he doesn't even know what a Core Study Unit is for history! He hasn't even bothered to read the document before he speaks to you!

Particularly interesting, though, were some teachers' responses to my asking whether externally-imposed or centrally-initiated factors – particularly those that resulted from implementation of policy imposed by the 1988 Education Reform Act (ERA) – affected their attitudes to the job. None of my interviewees had actually identified ERA-imposed factors as being significantly influential on their own job satisfaction, morale and motivation levels when I posed open-ended questions about how they felt about their jobs. It was clear from their comments that any impact which the national curriculum, for example, had had on their working lives had been superseded by that of school-specific issues, such as management and staff relations. Yet, my asking them to talk specifically about the national curriculum prompted responses which seemed to be intended to conform with the popular belief that its introduction has demoralized and demotivated teachers. It was almost as if these teachers felt they would be 'letting the side down' if they failed to identify the introduction of the national curriculum as a negative influence on teachers' job-related attitudes. In doing so, however, they seldom spoke subjectively; rather, they conveyed the impression that they were passing on second-hand knowledge. They did not refer to specific colleagues whom they knew to have been demoralized by the demands of the national curriculum, nor did their evaluations include reference to their own experiences. Moreover, when I probed deeper by asking if they could provide any subjective illustrations of how the introduction of the national curriculum had lowered their own morale or job satisfaction, most were unable to offer any, and those who were able to provide any, such as Pat, whose comments appear above, gave examples that only served to highlight the influence of negative school-specific factors. This was also the case with Rosemary. She could not think of any examples of how the introduction and the implementation of the national curriculum had adversely affected her own morale and job satisfaction, but her comments in her 1992 interview are illustrative of the generality with which complaints about the national curriculum were made. She responded to my asking her to move on to consideration of the extent to which centrally-imposed factors, such as pay, conditions of service and the introduction of the national curriculum, had influenced her morale and job satisfaction:

> I don't think pay really enters into it. If a pay rise comes along, everybody's happy. People can always use extra money, but ... er ... *I* think ... people would be happy with pay as it is – I don't think we've done too badly over these last few years, anyway; I think we've had *good* increases – a lot of other things have affected morale. ... I think ... you know ... the coming of the national curriculum. The thinking behind it was good ... er ... and you can understand why it was done ... but, the *way* it was done ... the speed ... er ... was all wrong, and this is what gets teachers' backs up more than anything. There've been so *many* changes in such a short time ... not only *those* changes, but, they're bringing changes to *those* changes ... for instance, the maths and the science. The dust has hardly settled ... people are just coming to terms with the national curriculum in maths and science, and the attainment targets are changing. So, it means a lot of changing and planning of the curriculum in school ... and it's these *changes* that people are not happy with. ... It *is* frustrating, and you feel sorry for the coordinators who put a lot of work in, and they write the policies, and they link it to the national curriculum, and then ... it's all changed. And so, they've got to re-write and ... er ... make changes. The same with the record-keeping, and the assessment. Er ... and I think there's a lot of criticism at both government and at county level, in that they don't give enough guidance. (Rosemary, Rockville teacher)

Positive influences on morale and job satisfaction were predominantly school-specific, as the following examples illustrate:

> Well, I enjoy the children; the sort of children that I work with ... and I like, to an extent, the freedom that you have in your own classroom. (Susan, Rockville teacher)

... but, I mean, when you get a child who comes in who's never been to school before – who can't even hold a pair of scissors, can't speak the language or anything ... and, within, say, six months you can watch them blossom and cope with things and ... you know ... the children ... the children are lovely! The children still have the magic that *our* children have lost. ... This, this 'awe' – this wonder of the world and the enthusiasm ... because *our* children are ... well, spoilt. ... But the Asian children have that real joy of everything you show them. I mean, at Eid [Muslim festival] we went to Smithfield Park, and, I mean, they should be used to it by now, but there was one little girl who'd never ever been in Smithfield Park! ... and, the flowers – she was just in absolute ecstasy! She just kept saying, 'Oh, the flowers ... the pretty flowers!' and she just went on and on ... she really was captivated with them. ... You'd have thought you'd given her the world! (Pat, Rockville teacher)

... the one thing at Leyburn, in many ways, is that there's a good social mix – partly because most of the teachers are from a working-class background – and there's lots of humour and experiences that we can all relate to ... like, a sense of humour ... *that's* important. (Mark, Leyburn teacher)

The reason why it is school-specific issues, situations and circumstances that evidently take precedence as morale-, motivation- and job satisfaction-influencing factors is that they constitute teachers' working lives. It is at the context-specific level that teachers carry out their work. Centrally-initiated conditions, or indeed any conditions that emanate from outside of the contexts in which teachers work, only become real for, and meaningful and relevant to, teachers when they become contextualized. Until they are effected within the contexts in which teachers work, such conditions are non-operational: they exist only in abstract form as ideas, principles or rhetoric. They do not constitute reality.

The introduction of the national curriculum does not, therefore, impact in a real sense upon teachers' lives until it is introduced into their contexts: their schools. The low status of teachers in society does not, as an issue, encroach upon a teacher's life until it is introduced into it, in the form of a derogatory remark or a perception of being unfavourably compared with other professionals. The problem of class sizes does not become a problem for teachers until it occurs in their own schools. It is only within the contexts of their own lives that things matter to people; although, sometimes, this contextualization may involve only consciousness and may not be dependent upon direct, activity-based experience. Under these circumstances, issues that, for example, are at odds with ideologies, offend sensibilities, or conflict with values – such as the plight of people living in war-torn Eastern Europe, famine in Africa, or, closer to home, the unfair treatment of a teacher whom one does not know, but whose case is reported in the media – are introduced into people's lives, and, therefore, realized, through contextualization.

It is also important to recognize that it is within the context in which teachers work that policy and initiatives that emanate from outside of this context begin, as they are implemented, to affect – positively or negatively – attitudes to the job. It is at school level that government-imposed reforms or Local Education Authority (LEA) or district initiatives may be put into operation in ways that are palatable to, or that alienate, teachers. Those who take responsibility for implementing externally-imposed change into schools have much capacity, through the institutionalization process that they adopt, for buffering teachers against, or conversely exposing them to, the worst anticipated effects of the changes. The buffering role is highlighted by McLaughlin *et al.* (1986, p. 425) who suggest that it should be taken on by school principals, district-level administrators and school board members. Externally-imposed change is never introduced into schools with a uniform level of intensity. Policy implementation varies from school to school. This was found to be the case with the introduction of the English and Welsh national curriculum. Evans *et al.*, (1994, pp. 100-106), reporting the findings of the Warwick study into the effects on teachers' lives of the introduction of the national curriculum, identify four approaches to implementation; the 'head-in-the-sand' approach, the 'paying lip service' approach, the 'common sense' approach, and the 'by the book' approach. Each approach reflected a different level of intensity of implementation, and, as such, affected with different levels of intensity the working lives of teachers. It is at school level, rather than at Whitehall, that teachers' working lives are affected.

The importance of leadership

This brings me to consideration of the issue, arising out of my research findings, that provides the impetus and that constitutes the rationale for this book: the influence of school leadership and management on teachers' attitudes to their jobs. It is, for the most part, leadership and management that define the school-specific contexts that affect teachers' working lives. My research findings revealed, categorically, that the greatest influences on teacher morale, job satisfaction and motivation are school leadership and management.

There is no doubt about it, headteachers have the capacity to make their staff dread going to work every Monday morning. They are capable of making teachers' working lives so unpleasant, or unfulfilling, or problematic, or frustrating, that they become the overriding reason why some members of staff move jobs. They may bring out the worst in people – antagonizing, engendering resentment, upsetting, demotivating – so that they never succeed in getting the very best out of the people whom they lead and manage.

Or, they may fire their staff with enthusiasm for their work, allow teachers to fulfil their potential, foster collegiality and cooperation, and make people reluctant to change jobs. Getting the best out of teachers begins at school level, not at central government level. This is becoming increasingly recognized by policy-makers in the UK. As I point out in the Introduction to this book, the national standards for headteachers (TTA, 1998) include some that focus on the motivation of staff, and the 1998 Green Paper (DfEE, 1998, para. 36) refers to the importance of headteachers motivating staff to 'give of their best'. More significantly, the motivational capacity of headteachers is spelled out by a Derbyshire secondary school headteacher's report in the *Guardian Education* (Stephens, 1998b) of his first-hand experience of getting the best out of teachers. Introduced with: 'Many teachers face poor prospects, low morale and even lower pay levels, but treat them right and they'll move mountains for you', Stephens' article begins:

> Society is suspicious of teachers and blames them for its ills. The job gets harder every year but remains poorly paid with diminishing prospects. The Government's proposals for the reform of the profession, announced this month, are potentially too divisive to be likely to help the situation.
>
> However, although it wouldn't solve every problem, teacher morale could be raised without cost if all heads were to start really caring for their teachers by adopting the following management advice . . .

Stephens then proceeds to list specific morale-raising management and leadership tips, all of which, without exception, reflect the kind of management and leadership that my research had revealed to be successful in engendering positive job-related attitudes amongst teachers.

It was school management and leadership of this kind that prompted one of my research interviewees, Helen, to say of one headteacher with whom she had worked:

> I don't know what it is about her, but she made you want to do your best – and not just for her, but for yourself. . . . You weren't working to please *her*, but she suddenly made you realize what was possible, and you, kind of, raised your game all the time.

Precisely what management of this kind involves, and how it may be achieved, are uncovered throughout the following chapters.

Notes

1 Fictitious names are used in all references to my research sample.

CHAPTER 2

A question of style

Introduction

The quotation from Helen at the end of the preceding chapter illustrates the motivating qualities of effective staff management. In contrast, Helen also referred, in her research interview, to her current headteacher and the effect which his leadership and management had upon her job-related attitudes, prompting her to seek – and secure – a new post:

> ... and although, yes, I've a lot of autonomy ... and I've thought, 'Why throw all this away? I've got my own little empire', but ... it wasn't enough ... Yes, the constraints are there, though. I'm just constrained by his apathy! ... If it's properly managed it's a very inspiring school to be in, but, at the moment ... it's not the school – it's the head. He's spoiling it. ... Other members of staff, like myself, who actually see things in a wider sense for the school, are getting out ... and I'm the last one to go.

The key question is: what was it about the headteacher to whom Helen referred in her first quotation that made her leadership so effective? If the secret of effective staff management lies in the leadership or management style that is adopted, then it is clearly important to identify the features of such a style. This chapter examines evidence from my own, and others', research of what it is about their headteachers and principals that motivates – or demotivates – staff. It considers what constitutes a motivational leadership style: what teachers want from their leaders.

School leadership styles

There has been a considerable amount of research carried out into the impact on staff of different leadership styles, within which are included studies in education contexts. Halpin's (1966) classic study of different organizational climates in American schools incorporates consideration of the leadership styles that were found to be integral to the different climates. The two extremes of Halpin's range of six organizational climates are what he refers to as the 'open' climate and the 'closed' climate. The 'open' climate headteacher is described as typically very enthusiastic, conscientious and hard-working, well-balanced in temperament, not aloof, and very much in control, albeit in a subtle manner. In this climate teachers are described as typically manifesting high morale, working collaboratively and seldom having cause for complaint. Schools with 'closed' climates are typically led by headteachers who are 'highly aloof and impersonal', who emphasize the need for hard work but fail themselves to work hard and who say one thing and do another. Teachers working in 'closed' climates, according to Halpin, do not work well together, derive little satisfaction from their work, and dislike their headteacher.

Ball (1987, p. 83) describes a leadership style as 'a form of social accomplishment, a particular way of realizing and enacting the authority of headship'. He identifies four leadership styles that emerged in the course of his research in British secondary schools: the *interpersonal* and *managerial* styles and the *political* style, which he subdivides into the *adversarial* and the *authoritarian* styles.

The interpersonal head is described as typically 'mobile' and 'visible', with a preference for consulting with individuals rather than holding meetings. S/he likes to 'sound out ideas' and 'gather opinion' (Ball, 1987, p. 88). 'Such heads will frequently reiterate to staff the importance of bringing complaints and grievances to them first of all; "my door is always open", they will say' (Ball, 1987, p. 90). Ball suggests that this style of leadership is particularly effective at satisfying teachers' individual needs, and that grievances and staff turnover tend to remain low. Yet, since interpersonal heads are often perceived to be influenced by individual members of staff, resentment may be engendered. Moreover, since there are usually no formal and visible decision-making mechanisms in place under such leadership – 'Decision-making is not focused. There is no one place or moment when decisions are made' (Ball, 1987, p. 93) – teachers may feel frustrated and insecure.

Managerial heads, Ball writes (1987, p. 96), adopt a style of leadership that parallels that of industry managers:

> The use of management techniques involves the importation into the school of structures, types of relationships and processes of organizational control from the factory. The managerial head is chief executive of the school, normally surrounded and supported by a senior management team ... The head relates to the staff through this team ... and through a formal

structure of meetings and committees. Both these responsibilities and structures will be supported and outlined by written documentation which specifies terms of reference and job descriptions.

Ball's research revealed several deficiencies of a managerial leadership style: a sense of exclusion from decision-making on the part of those teachers who are not members of the senior management team, the creation of a 'them and us' hierarchically-based division, and teachers' derision for the management structure and its processes.

The adversarial leadership style is typified by confrontational dialogue between the head and teachers: 'They speak of "rows", "battles", "challenges". Here, then, headship is very much a public performance; the emphasis is upon persuasion and commitment' (Ball, 1987, p. 104). Adversarial heads' preoccupation is with issues that reflect ideologies, rather than administration and procedures. They typically focus discussion on the quality of education provided in the school and on whether the institution is fulfilling its purpose. Teachers' responses to this style of leadership, Ball (1987, p. 104) suggests, are mixed:

> Some staff will be unable or unwilling to participate in this form of organizational discourse. Some find it unhelpful or unconducive, others are unwilling to devote to it the time and energy that is necessary to 'get your point of view across'.

Authoritarian leadership is distinct from adversarial leadership by its focus on asserting rather than persuading:

> Such a head takes no chances by recognizing the possibility of competing views and interests. Opposition is avoided, disabled or simply ignored. No opportunities are provided for the articulation of alternative views or the assertion of alternative interests, other than those defined by the head as legitimate. Indeed, the authoritarian may rely, as a matter of course, on conscious deception as a matter of organizational control. (Ball, 1987, p. 109)

In response to authoritarianism, Ball found that teachers typically either acquiesced – generally because they felt intimidated – or confronted the head and disputed decisions. In the latter case there was limited chance of success on the part of teachers, since one of the key features of authoritarian leadership is to deflect opposition. This engendered anger and frustration with the inevitable futility of posing challenges to policy and decisions.

In her study of British primary school teachers' job satisfaction, Nias (1980) identified three dimensions of leadership style: initiating structure, consideration and decision-centralization. These refer respectively to the extent to which leaders define and structure their own and their subordinates' roles towards attaining goals; the extent to which leaders manifest concern, support and respect for their staff; and the extent to which leaders influence group decisions. Nias found that the individual school leaders in her study could be positioned differently along each of these three dimensions, and that the resulting spread revealed what she categorized as three leadership styles: the passive, positive, and Bourbon types, which she describes:

> One leadership type, the 'passive', gave teachers more freedom than they desired. They perceived themselves as totally free to set their own goals, under heads whose professional standards did not match their own, and who offered neither coherence to the school as a whole nor support and guidance to individuals. The second, the 'Bourbon', was characterized by social distance, authoritarian professional relationships, and administrative efficiency. The third, which I have described as 'positive', set teachers a high professional standard, adopted a dynamic but consultative policy towards decision-making, and actively supported the professional development of individuals. (Nias, 1980, p. 261)

In relation to teachers' job satisfaction, Nias found 'passive' and 'Bourbon' heads to have the most negative, and 'positive' heads the most positive, influence: 'A "positive" style ... provided the context in which a keen teacher could get on with his chosen work and therefore contributed considerably to his job satisfaction' (Nias, 1980, p. 270).

What do teachers want from their leaders?

Which of the leadership styles described in this chapter seems most likely to foster positive attitudes in teachers? Which, in particular, seems to have the greatest motivating potential? This outline review of research evidence highlights some of the positive and negative features of the different ways in which headteachers handle staff. It does not, however, indicate emphatically which, of the leadership styles identified, is the one that is most likely to motivate teachers. It does not provide a blueprint for leadership that is guaranteed to get the best out of staff.

So, what *do* teachers want from their leaders? What are the features of leadership that fires them with enthusiasm, sustains them, and gets them – in the terminology used by my interviewee, Helen – trying to raise their game all the time? In order to address these questions, I now present and discuss some of the findings from my own research.

One of the studies that I carried out (see Appendix) was a case study of morale, job satisfaction and motivation at Rockville County

Primary School (see Evans, 1998, pp. 60-1, for full background details about the school). Rockville was led by Geoff Collins, whose management of the school and its staff, and the effect that this had on teachers' attitudes to their work, are well worth examining for the valuable insight they provide.

The impression that I gained of Geoff Collins, the Rockville head, throughout my prolonged attachment at the school, matched the consensual perception of the Rockville teachers who participated in my research as interviewees. Geoff was seen as a very affable, essentially well-meaning, but weak head who avoided difficulties and confrontation and allowed himself to be governed and dominated by one or two strong personalities amongst the staff. His management style was the subject of considerable derision; indeed it was generally agreed that he was an exceptionally poor manager.

In relation to the leadership styles identified above, it is very difficult to categorize Geoff. Ball (1987, p. 116) points out that not all heads may fit into the typology of styles that he presents, and that some heads will manifest a combination of styles. The latter certainly seems to have been true in Geoff's case. He displayed many features of Ball's interpersonal leadership style; indeed, he seemed to thrive on interpersonal relationships. In a pastoral-type role he appeared to be concerned about the well-being of all of his colleagues equally, as individuals. He endeavoured to maintain good relations with everyone, tried to please as many people as possible, was never bad-tempered, never criticized and was, essentially, mild-mannered at all times. He manifested a degree of equanimity and goodwill which precluded his ever, to my knowledge, falling out with anyone; indeed, it seemed impossible to fall out with him since he brushed off snubs, insults and criticism and refused to be drawn into arguments. He avoided conflict, and always tried to allow his sunny disposition and geniality to fight off ill-feeling, dismissing complaints, whenever he was able to, with a joking response. He evidently preferred, in relation to policy issues and staff grievances, to conduct one-to-one discussions rather than handle group meetings. He liked to sound out ideas and 'test the water', and seemed to use informal one-to-one or small group discussions as a vehicle for trying to win support for controversial decisions.

Geoff was very sociable, and enjoyed one-to-one discussions and chats with any of his colleagues. His fundamentally caring approach to individuals was demonstrated by his often going out of his way to help colleagues who had personal crises or difficulties. Yet, his concern to avoid conflict brought out in Geoff managerial behaviour that reflects aspects of the authoritarian style identified by Ball (1987, p. 109). In particular, Geoff was, on several occasions, perceived to have deliberately misled – even, it was reported by some of my interviewees, blatantly lied to – teachers.

In other respects, Geoff exhibited characteristics of Ball's managerial leadership style. He had established a senior management team consisting of himself, Margaret, the deputy head, and Alison, who was the next most senior teacher and who had been placed in charge of what was then known as the school's infants (now Key Stage 1: ages 5-7) department. Geoff's attitude to management seemed very clearly to be one of blind faith, non-intervention and unquestioning support in relation to those of his colleagues who held promoted posts, even at the lowest level of the promotion hierarchy, but particularly within the senior management team. This attitude was applied, without exception, to incumbents of promoted posts, not in a personal capacity, but in their capacity as post-holders. Since its hierarchically-oriented, rather than personally-oriented, basis was recognized it was not interpreted as favouritism, but its unquestioning, and often evidently irrational, basis created much frustration and resentment. Geoff manifested this attitude to management by his apparently blinkered, 'head-in-the-sand' manner of refusing to accept criticism of the behaviour, policies and decisions of teachers who held posts of responsibility, particularly those who constituted his senior management team. I recall, for example, overhearing a conversation with a Rockville teacher during my teaching-cum-observing. The teacher had complained to Geoff at having been left alone to teach a large class of reception children (aged 4 and 5) when her co-teacher was sick and when she had seen Alison, the head of the infants' department, who did not have responsibility for a class of her own, coming and going throughout the morning on seemingly routine, non-teaching tasks: filling flower vases, stocking bookshelves and transferring the contents of one cupboard to another. She had asked Geoff why Alison had not assigned herself to assist in what she knew to be the understaffed reception class, and she had questioned the deployment of the senior teacher during the rest of that day. Geoff's response was characteristically courteous, but unwavering: Alison was, he said, a senior teacher who had been given responsibility and who was to carry out that responsibility as she saw fit. He would not make Alison accountable for her movements, nor would he assign her to help in the reception class. The issue was not debatable, and the message conveyed by Geoff, on this and on many similar occasions, was clear: there was no right of appeal against decisions made by senior members of staff.

Yet, Geoff was also a *laissez-faire* head who manifested many – though not all – of the characteristics of Nias' (1980) 'passive' head. Perhaps reflecting his evident reluctance to criticize and his concern to avoid confrontation, he allowed teachers considerable autonomy. Indeed, he failed to manifest a clear vision of the direction in which he wanted the school to move. For the most part, Geoff's educational beliefs were not made explicit. Many teachers remarked that they had no sense of what his views were on teaching and learning methods, curriculum development, or indeed any educational issues. Some implied that he had no strong views at all on such matters. He simply did not convey any impression of having applied any depth of analysis to any issues of this kind. He appeared to be oblivious to the activities that went on in classrooms and never commented on specific projects. He just allowed teachers to teach precisely as they liked, unhindered, and, to a large extent, unobserved by him.

During research interviews the Rockville staff spoke candidly and were, in most cases, highly critical of Geoff's management of the school:

> I think he finds the management role incredibly difficult ... to say he's been on two management courses ... you'd think he'd realize that he wasn't a manager. (Susan, Rockville teacher)

> I think he thinks he's doing his best ... which, I think, he is ... in his way ... but, whether it's the right way for the school is arguable, really, you see. ... And, certainly, his management skills leave a lot to be desired. (Deborah, Rockville school secretary)

> He's not directing the school – it's the tail wagging the dog! ... He's in the wrong job – his personality's wrong for this kind of job. (Hilary, ESL[1] teacher based at the Language Centre housed at Rockville)

> I think he'd probably say himself that ... he's not a manager. (Brenda, Rockville teacher)

During the course of my research, there arose a situation concerning the deployment of senior teachers which gave rise to widespread condemnation of Geoff's hierarchical managerial approach and which undermined his credibility as headteacher more than any other situation or event of which I was aware. Having established a management team, Geoff then developed a policy of freeing-up the time of his two most senior colleagues in order to increase their availability for management tasks. This involved the senior teachers not having class responsibilities, but being deployed as support teachers. At first, each of them kept to a timetable which deployed them fairly equitably amongst the different classes and left one afternoon free for management duties, but the situation gradually evolved over several months whereby Margaret, the deputy head,

abandoned her timetable in favour of operating a system of supporting teachers on a more *ad hoc* basis. This change was announced by
Margaret herself, with Geoff's approval, at a staff meeting which I
attended. Margaret explained how, in future, if no one objected, she
would make day-to-day assessments of teachers' needs and deploy
herself as she considered appropriate. This would give her greater
flexibility, she argued, and was much more workable than rigid
timetabling, which had often had to be abandoned when conflicting
demands on her time arose.

Whilst, ostensibly, Margaret's initiative was accepted in the meeting,
it was heavily criticized in many closeted discussions over the following
days. Margaret was generally perceived as a forthright, assertive, even,
on occasions, aggressive personality who greatly influenced policy by
dominating Geoff. Her plans for a discretionary system of self-
deployment were greeted with suspicion and generally interpreted as
carte blanche for her to do what she liked, when she liked.

This initial cynicism proved to be justified as, gradually, Margaret's
decisions about which teachers to support, the activities that she
undertook in classes, and her movements in general, began to be
questioned and criticized. Amongst themselves at first, teachers
complained, for example, that Margaret was becoming increasingly
elusive, that she only went into the classes of teachers whom she liked
and to whom she related well, that she typically did not teach in any
capacity but often only sat and observed or wandered around chatting to children and looking at their work. There were also
increasingly frequent reports of her having failed to appear in any
classrooms at all. On these occasions she was often seen chatting at
length in the corridors, or sitting in the staffroom drinking coffee.
One of my interviewees described the situation:

> We don't seem to know where she [Margaret] went. This was a question in
> everybody's minds – 'Where *was* she?' ... When we discussed this in the
> staffroom Margaret hadn't been in to other classrooms ... at other times of
> the day she'd been seen going over to the infants' building, but nobody
> seems to know where she was *there*. (Elaine, Rockville teacher)

Let us, at this point, consider what are likely to be the attitudinal
responses of the Rockville teachers to this issue of the deployment of
the deputy head. In my description of what unfolded I have already
given some indication of teachers' initial reactions. Consider,
though, what might be the more long-term effect on their job-related
attitudes. It is not unreasonable to expect manifestations of dissatisfaction with the prevailing situation, nor is it unreasonable to
expect staff morale and, in some cases, motivation to be adversely
affected.

Consider, also, what course of action the Rockville teachers ought to have taken if, indeed, they were dissatisfied – for whatever reasons – with the deputy head's apparent abrogation of her responsibilities and failure to do the job for which she was being paid. One of the most obvious courses of action would be to have raised the matter with the headteacher and communicated to him their dissatisfaction. Consider, then, how the headteacher might have responded to complaints about his deputy – complaints of a serious nature: that for some time she had evidently failed to do any teaching at all. Consider, first, what you would have done if you had been the Rockville head faced with this situation. Then consider how, based on the descriptions that I have presented of his management style, Geoff Collins would have been likely to respond. Bear in mind, in particular, Geoff's concern to avoid trouble and confrontation, and his dogmatic refusal to accept criticism of any member of his senior management team.

What actually occurred was that, since it became apparent, as the situation persisted for several months, that Geoff either was oblivious to it or was not prepared to do anything to alter it, some teachers raised the issue with him. This was not done in the form of a deputation, but by individuals or very small groups communicating their concerns informally. Some of those who had complained to Geoff spoke of this in their research interviews:

> I said, 'That's what a lot of the staff are complaining about – you know, that Margaret's floating around doing nothing', and I said, 'To me, she should have a timetable . . . and she should be relieving teachers as well.'
> *Interviewer. And how did he react to this?*
> (mimicking Geoff) 'Oh, well, oh, we can't have any of that – no non-contact time. Oh, no!' It's just something you don't have, to Geoff – apart from when you get quarter of an hour for assembly, or something like that.
> (Jane, Rockville teacher)

> A deputy head should have all the responsibilities of a class teacher, *plus* others . . . but the deputy head in our school has no curricular responsibilities, no class . . . you know. . . . He [Geoff] has allowed the management team to make up their own job descriptions . . . and these new conditions of service haven't been applied to them – he's just applied them to everybody else.
> *Interviewer. Why do you, or any of you, not try and tackle Geoff directly about this?*
> I think we have.
> *Interviewer. And what's been the result?*
> Nothing . . . there hasn't been any. (Susan, Rockville teacher)

From all accounts, Geoff's response to being apprised of the situation of Margaret's deployment was, characteristically, one of non-intervention. Moreover, several teachers spoke of his having defended the policy of Margaret's self-discretionary deployment and fobbing off teachers who complained to him. Many were convinced that Geoff did not wish to know about the problem and they interpreted his response as reflecting a head-in-the-sand attitude:

> He [Geoff] will listen ... and you think he's taken in some of your points ... but, in the end, he goes his own way, and I think this is what happened over Margaret, when we had to say, 'Well, it's not good for a deputy head to be seen sitting in the hall, just after Comic Relief week, counting money while the other staff are teaching. If somebody came into school and saw that ... '. 'Oh, I didn't know about that,' he says. But when he *did* know about it, because we'd told him, he still didn't think much of it. ... Janet Bradshaw complained about her – so he knew about it – but, weeks later, when Joanne and I went and complained about something else ... he treats it as news – as if he's just heard it. He seemed to be aware of the problems, but he just cut himself off. (Elaine, Rockville teacher)

What transpired, then, was that, whilst Margaret's behaviour attracted condemnation from the growing number of teachers who noticed it, and who aired their disapproval in small groups behind closed doors, it was Geoff who provoked the greater outrage with his characteristic *laissez-faire*, or passive, response. Whilst a façade of good relations was maintained between Margaret and the rest of the staff, a core group of teachers was becoming increasingly discontented with Geoff's tacit acceptance of what they considered to be Margaret's inappropriate deployment, and with what several reported as his refusal to address the issue when it was brought to his attention.

The issue of the deputy head's deployment remained for what the Rockville teachers estimate to be two years, before Geoff's hand was forced by two teachers, Joanne and Elaine, who had decided that enough was enough, and who brought matters to a head by threatening to make an official complaint to the LEA's Director of Education:

> Well, Joanne and I went to him, twice – two lunch-time sessions with him. We just told him straight ... it wasn't good for the school. I think *now* he realizes. (Elaine, Rockville teacher)

The school secretary also described the events that prompted Geoff to make a positive response:

> *Interviewer: So what happened about this Margaret business, then? Did the staff confront him? Was it **all** the staff, or just some?*
> No ... not *all* the staff, no ... well, he kept talking to me ... oh, well – you know what he's like – for ages ... and then ... I think he felt it was one of those problems that would go away, you see. ... Well, Elaine and Joanne were what I call the ringleaders – well, for want of a better word – because they're the most articulate and loudest-spoken. They saw Geoff, and

Joanne – well, both – they both asked me to go and sit with them one dinner time, and they put forward what the staff had said ... and they wanted something doing ... er ... something decisive ... er, you know ... they were trying to get him to get it sorted out. (Deborah, Rockville school secretary)

The outcome was that Margaret, who by this time had been diagnosed as suffering from a nervous illness, took early retirement on the grounds of ill health. Her successor, though, and Alison, the infants' department head, continued, at Geoff's insistence, to be floating teachers without class responsibilities.

The point of my relating these events, and of describing the prevailing situation at Rockville that concerned the deployment of the deputy head, is to apply consideration of them in order to develop deeper understanding of the impact of management on teachers' attitudes to their work. What lessons are to be learned from the Rockville case? What does it tell us about the effects of leadership styles on staff morale, job satisfaction and motivation?

Let us consider first Geoff Collins' leadership style. How might it be described? I have already suggested that his leadership reflects a combination of styles. In particular, of the leadership styles outlined in this chapter, Geoff may perhaps best be described as predominantly a passive head who adopted what was, for the most part, an interpersonal style of leadership. This is only an approximation, though. In the first place, Geoff was not entirely passive. He was perceived by all of his staff to be very stubborn on many occasions and in relation to certain issues. All of my interviewees made reference to his tendency to 'dig his heels in' over matters that he considered particularly important. Under these circumstances, they all agreed, he could never be persuaded or dissuaded: it was impossible to sway him. Indeed, this trait manifested itself most clearly though his intransigence over the issue of the deployment of senior teachers. In the second place, he did not display all of the characteristics identified by Ball (1987) as those belonging to interpersonal leaders. As we have seen, Geoff was not, for example, particularly effective at satisfying teachers' individual needs. Moreover, though he might have been justified in claiming that his door was always open and that he was ready to listen to complaints and grievances, he might just as well have kept his door closed since, from all accounts, he often failed to respond to teachers' expressions of dissatisfaction.

This raises the issue of whether, in fact, examination of leadership styles offers anything useful to understanding staff management. My view is that it is of very limited use, and my choice of title for this chapter – which is a play on the use of the word 'question' – reflects this view. The identification of school leadership styles reflects educational sociologists' tendencies towards presenting research findings as typologies. Since typologies constitute generalizations, though, they inevitably exclude much. In the particular case of school leadership style typologies, my own research – as well as my anecdotal evidence – yields very few examples that conform to an approximation of a single style. Certainly, there are many examples of style *combinations*, but even these – as in the case of the Rockville head – exemplify only certain specific style components, and represent so complex a combination that their relationship to any one identified leadership style becomes quite tenuous. The reason for this, I believe, is that leadership styles involve only interactive behavioural processes. They do not incorporate consideration of other factors that are relevant to leader-staff interaction, such as intellectual compatibility and the extent to which values and ideologies are shared. My research revealed these factors to be important influences on leadership success. It is not simply the more observable features of leadership that are useful in furthering understanding of what does and does not work. These present an incomplete picture, and yet these are, for the most part, what constitute a 'style'. The part of the picture that is missing is that provided by information about what makes a leader act as s/he does towards staff, or in relation to policy- and decision-making: information such as what her/his educational ideologies are; how intelligent or knowledgeable s/he is; what vision for the school s/he has. This part of the picture makes the way in which a specific leadership style is effected have variable impact upon staff. The impact upon staff of an interpersonal leadership style practised by an intelligent, well-informed, knowledgeable, 'on-the-ball' head is likely to be very different from the impact of the same basic style effected by a head whose outlook is narrow, who is set in her/his ways, whose knowledge is inadequate and who does not manifest a particularly high intellectual level.

In relation to understanding how leaders may get the best out of their staff, I suggest that it is likely to be more useful to identify and examine – as I try to do in this book – first, ideologically-based frameworks for fostering positive leader-staff interaction and, second, individual, specific 'units' of interactive behaviour – what might, when they are prescriptive, be called leadership behaviour 'tips' – than try to group these as identifiable styles.

Let us now assess the impact upon the Rockville staff of the headteacher's handling of the issue of the deputy head's deployment. At first glance – and, certainly, based on the evidence that I have presented so far – it may appear that the impact was to lower staff morale, create extensive dissatisfaction and, in some cases, demotivate. More evidence that this was the case is provided by the comments made by Rockville interviewees:

> *Interviewer. If you were given the chance of going to another school . . . would you jump at it, or would you be more selective, or what? How desperate are you to get out, in other words?*
> Oh, yes! I'd go to an infants' school – just infants.
> *Interviewer. And what is it, basically . . . is it just **one** thing that's driving you out . . . is it the management – the hierarchy, that you've spoken of . . . or is it a lot of other things?*
> Well . . . waste of . . . er . . . waste of manpower, I think a lot of it is. (Jean, Rockville teacher)

> Well, I would say that my morale at the moment is lower than average . . . because of all the stresses and strains of various things that've been going on.
> *Interviewer. Yes. Can you elaborate?*
> Yes . . . mainly with the deputy . . . not doing the job she was supposed to be doing . . . the pressure on other staff . . . everybody's feeling it and, of course, everybody's discussing it, which tends to bring morale down . . . negative views on things . . . I don't think she went round visiting class-rooms as it was claimed she did. (Elaine, Rockville teacher)

> I mean, it's disgusting! I mean, she [Margaret] does have a timetable now, but it's *so* ambiguous and so flexible, it's just beyond . . . beyond reason! . . . Well, to say we've got all these managers, how can the school *be* so mismanaged – it's a farce! (Pat, Rockville teacher)

Yet comments such as these do not illustrate the full picture. The most striking, overall finding to emerge from the Rockville study was the diversity of job-related attitudinal responses. In relation to the issue of the deployment of staff, for example, and in particular that of the deputy head, despite unanimous recognition of the situation amongst my interviewees, the effect which it had on job satisfaction, morale and motivation varied considerably. Although there was general, increasingly widespread dissatisfaction over the issue, it is also the case that levels of, and the reasons underlying the, dissatisfaction varied. It was a majority of teachers who were clearly very dissatisfied with what they considered to be an unacceptable situation, but there was also a reasonably large minority of more tolerant or complacent views. Several interviewees, like Rosemary and Stephen, whose comments are presented below, clearly had managed to detach themselves sufficiently from the situation to allow them to cope with it by not allowing it to impact too negatively on their attitudes to their work:

> I think changes are planned for a more efficient carrying out of the deputy headship role . . . and it's not before time, because this has been the root of

a lot of staff's dissatisfaction ... this drifting around. ... That's when dissatisfaction began to creep in. ... I think that was the beginning of it ... the thing just went from bad to worse ... and I think a lot of people ... er ... felt very low at that point, and, you know, feelings were running high. *Interviewer: And how did* **you** *feel at this point? Did it bother you?* Not *personally*, because ... I'd, sort of, organized myself and was getting on with the job that I felt I was employed to do ... er ... and I didn't really let it ... er ... bother me. I mean, Margaret was timetabled to come into the reception class, but we never ever saw her ... only on very, very rare occasions when she just breezed in. ... So, personally, you know, I didn't let it get to me, because, if you recall, when you were there, people were getting to the point where something had to be done ... either *they* had to get out, or they'd to bring in some outside help to remedy things there ... and, you know, people were talking about going down to the Education Office, and, you know, they had no confidence in management, and so on. ... But, I didn't really want to get involved in that because ... er ... I don't know – maybe I'm a bit of a coward ... er ... I didn't want any more ill-feeling within the place than there already was ... and, also, I felt sorry for Geoff in a lot of ways because, as I say, he was a victim of circumstances ... er ... I really think he was up against a very confident and a very tough ... and aggressive ... person ... and I think he had to tread very carefully, otherwise, you know, perhaps he could have been destroyed by it. (Rosemary, Rockville teacher)

Interviewer: People have criticized the way in which there are two members of staff who don't have classes ... now, how does this affect **you** *?*
Er, it doesn't, really – I wouldn't say it affected me all *that* much. ... No, it doesn't get on my nerves as much as it gets on other people's nerves ... things like that don't really get to me as much, I don't think ... er ... if they haven't got a class. (Stephen, Rockville teacher)

As these illustrative comments show, responses to the issue of the deployment of senior staff were wide-ranging. It was particularly interesting that this diversity of attitudinal response did not seem to be a straightforward case of multiple perceptions. As is shown by the samples of illustrative quotes presented throughout this chapter, there was general agreement in relation to what was going on in the school, even between teachers representing the extreme levels of morale and job satisfaction. It was, therefore, not perceptions but responses which were diverse. Situations and circumstances which were clearly acknowledged by all who were aware of them as undesirable did not necessarily, in all cases, lower morale nor give rise to significant dissatisfaction. This calls into question the validity of the notion of whole school morale, and reveals both job satisfaction and morale to be essentially individual phenomena, as I explain in Chapter 1. In their study of different positive school cultures, Nias *et al.* (1989) found a similar trend of diversity within each of the schools examined: 'We need to stress that in none of the schools were staff

groups homogeneous or totally cohesive' (p. 47). This issue highlights yet another limitation of the applicability of the study of
leadership styles, arising out of neglect of consideration of the
important dimension of the individuality of teachers. What teachers
want from their leaders is not simple and straightforward to ascertain
because, in any group of teachers, there are likely to be individuals
who each want different things. Quite simply, in relation to leadership, what suits one teacher may not suit another.

Teachers' preferences: accounting for the differences

My research has revealed three key interrelated factors – all of which
stem from biographical factors – that underpin teachers' leadership-
related preferences. I refer to these as teachers' professionality
orientations, relative perspectives and realistic expectations. Precisely what I mean by 'professionality orientation' is explained fully
in the next chapter so it will suffice here to refer to it concisely as the
extent to which teachers' professional values and practice are
informed by rationality, reflection and a theoretical knowledge base.
The relative perspectives factor concerns how teachers view their
school's leadership in relation to other factors. Such perspectives
incorporate prioritization and comparison and are seldom static, but
will tend to fluctuate in response to re-prioritization and re-evalua-
tion which may result from changed and changing circumstances
and experiences. Hoppock (1977) identified this factor in his pion-
eering survey, conducted in 1933,' of job satisfaction amongst all
adult residents of New Hope, Pennsylvania:

> The New Hope Survey was made four years after the panic of 1929 and
> before there were any very promising indications of recovery. Millions were
> unemployed. Presumably anyone who had a job was grateful for it and
> anxious to keep it ... in other words, satisfaction may be a function of
> relative status: when the individual is better off than his neighbors he is
> satisfied and when he is worse off he is dissatisfied. (Hoppock, 1977,
> p. 10)

Factors which determine how teachers consider the leadership of
their schools include comparative experiences, comparative insights,
and the circumstances and events which make up the rest of their
lives: their non-work selves. Teachers view and place the way in which
they are led as it relates to factors such as these. Comparative
experiences, for example, could be previous jobs, or having worked
with different headteachers; comparative insights may include
knowledge of how another school is run; and the relativity arising out
of consideration of their non-teaching lives would involve the prioritization which is a prerequisite of putting the job into perspective. If,

for example, teachers afford their work low priority within the rest of their lives, they are less likely – on the whole – to be affected by the ways in which their schools are led than are teachers for whom work is the most important part of their lives. This kind of distinction is illustrated clearly by comparing two Rockville teachers' views on Geoff Collins' leadership. Amanda, who took her work very seriously and afforded it very high priority in her life, spoke of the leadership at Rockville:

> I suppose, in a sense, Geoff as headteacher was no longer credible. . . . I'll be honest with you . . . I am absolutely *dreading* – well, I shan't go back to Rockville . . . I shan't go back after this secondment . . . I shall have to look for a different sort of work if I can't – I can't go back there, and I can't, any more, tolerate . . . er . . . I can't tolerate a shoddy performance!

Brenda's relative perspective, on the other hand, allowed her to evaluate Geoff Collins' leadership much more favourably:

> *Interviewer. Did this situation ever bother you at all . . . or are you the sort of person who thinks, 'Well, I'll get on with **my** job and they can do what they like'?*
> I think, again, it very much depends on how you feel – I mean, if I was a career teacher . . . if I was going – I mean, say, like Susan Ashcroft, or somebody like that, who obviously wants to get on – er . . . I think then, probably, I would feel much more strongly about it. . . . I just think that, now . . . in the last four or five years – I suppose it's a maturity – the things that mattered before don't matter now. . . . I'm just interested, basically, in living each day for the day, and being happy with it . . . and happy with what I'm doing. I'm probably very complacent now, but . . . alright, I'm complacent. . . . *Most* women can't do with somebody who's incredibly tolerant and lets everybody be happy. . . . As a person, I respect Geoff . . . but, er . . . I think on the whole, a lot of women together can't do with someone like Geoff. . . . But, why should it make any difference what the head's like? . . . It doesn't make any difference to *me*. . . . I don't see why the head *should* bother you . . . because, really, Geoff has very little influence on *me*.

The outcome of having a relative perspective of how they are led at work is that teachers, having compared their current leadership favourably or unfavourably with the factors which constitute their evaluative yardstick, are able to rate it as either relatively satisfactory or unsatisfactory. At Rockville, teachers for whom the school's leadership represented, for example, an improvement upon their previous work-related situations viewed it relatively favourably and were, predictably, less dissatisfied than were those of their colleagues who perceived Geoff Collins' leadership as representing a deterioration in work-related conditions.

Teachers' realistic expectations of their work contexts and situations, including school leadership, do not necessarily reflect their 'ideals', but, rather, those expectations which they feel are realistically able to be fulfilled. Chase (1953) became aware of the

importance of expectations through one of the earliest studies of
teacher morale, a questionnaire survey of nearly 1800 American
teachers: 'When teachers' expectations are fulfilled with regard to
the leadership of administrators and supervisors, their morale soars;
when their expectations are disappointed, morale takes a nose dive'
(Chase, 1953, p. 1).

Such expectations reflect values and ideologies, and will be partly
influenced by professionality and comparative experiences and
insights. In this way, the three factors that I identify as underlying the
diversity of attitudinal responses to the work context and to school
leadership – professionality, relative perspective, and realistic expectations – are clearly interrelated. Essentially, individuals differ – for
all sorts of reasons – in relation to what they expect of those who lead
them. The extent to which these realistic expectations of leaders are
fulfilled is an important influence on teachers' job-related attitudes.
At Rockville, for example, the headteacher's loss of credibility to
Amanda stemmed from a series of incidents that reflected his failure
to meet her expectations of him. Geoff did not conform to Amanda's
view of what school headship involves. In her research interview,
Amanda related one particular incident:

> Er ... well ... the second term that I was there I had instances with two
> children ... er ... and one child in particular who ... er ... needed a
> remedial reading programme. Now ... er ... I didn't know how to go about
> broaching this, and so I did it, sort of, generally, in conversation with Geoff
> Collins, and he said I'd only to mention it and it would be attended to. ...
> Now, I mentioned it and nothing was done about it.
> *Interviewer: You mentioned it to whom?*
> I had to mention it to Margaret Kitchen. ... Nothing was done about it and
> so, as time went on, I became more and more open in what I was saying to
> him and less subtle, I suppose. ... And so ... er ... he then said *he* would
> mention it to Margaret, that I had a child ... and she came and she had one
> hour with this child and left me a box of stuff and she said she'd come back
> the next day. And she never came back again, and that stuff was on my
> window sill for two terms. So, when I *said* what had happened I assumed
> that Geoff would do something about it, and I told him there was no small
> group work going on. So, he knew about it and did nothing about it. Well,
> when I say, 'did nothing about it' – nothing *happened*. So I realized that ...
> er ... he may honestly have believed what he'd told me was happening but,
> when he knew it wasn't ... er ...
> *Interviewer: ... he would rectify it?*
> Yes – and it didn't happen.

Similarly, at Sefton Road Primary – another of the schools in which I
carried out research – Louise's expectations of Phil, the headteacher,
were not met. As Louise's comments suggest, the Sefton Road
context was starkly different from the Rockville context, and her
unfavourable evaluation of Phil's leadership was quite distinct from

most of her colleagues', highlighting, again, the importance of the individuality-of-teachers dimension to leadership success:

> ... if I'd been at Sefton Road when I was actually assessed for my proba-
> tionary year I just couldn't have coped. I believe Phil has you doing lesson
> plans *all the time* when you're a probationer – whereas I only did them
> when the adviser was coming in.
> ... And I feel that, with Phil, he wants 110 per cent off everybody ... and I
> think that's asking too much.

Developing leadership that motivates

To those who want to motivate staff and lead in ways that get the best out of everyone it is rather unhelpful simply to point out that teachers differ in relation to what motivates them. Certainly, since teachers want different things from their leaders, developing motivational leadership is not straightforward. It may appear that teachers' expectations of leadership are diverse and that, as a result, it is impossible to satisfy everyone. This is not entirely the case. It *is* the case that, as a leader – whether you are a headteacher or principal, departmental or faculty head, team leader or coordinator of an area of the curriculum – you will not be able to satisfy everyone all of the time. We have already seen that there does not seem to be one single style of leadership that provides a model for effective motivation – although, clearly, some styles appear more effective than others. Yet, it is important to realize that, although on the surface they may differ in their expectations and preferences, funda- mentally teachers – like anyone else – are uniform. They are uniform in wanting their needs to be met. The key to managing to motivate, therefore, is to offer leadership that accommodates individuals' diverse needs, and throughout this book I examine ways of doing this.

It is also important to realize that, although teachers are individ- uals, it is nevertheless possible to identify generalizable character- istics that apply to some teachers. By this process, loose categories or broad groups of teachers emerge who share similar perspectives, values, ideologies, expectations and job-related preferences and who, therefore, are motivated in similar ways. The leader who wants to motivate as many staff as possible will clearly gain a lot by under- standing the needs of these groups of teachers. The next chapter focuses upon one such group: 'extended' professionals.

Note

1 English as a second language.

CHAPTER 3

Talent spotting: Getting the best out of 'extended' professionals

Introduction

Imagine you are a member of a selection panel considering which of two primary teachers to appoint to your inner-city, multiracial school. The two teachers in question are called Joanne and Amanda. They both have the same qualifications. They both have extensive experience of teaching socially disadvantaged children, including ethnic minority ESL children. They both seem pleasant and amiable and are likely to fit in well with the staff peer group. They both appear efficient and well-organized. They both have very good references. They both appear to have the qualities and experience that you are looking for in a new appointee. So, which one do you choose?

To help you decide, you will need to know something more about Joanne and Amanda. You will want to know what kind of teacher each of them is, what their views are on certain educational issues, and how each approaches the business of teaching a class. To find out this information you would raise pertinent questions at the job interview.

Imagine, then, that in their interviews you ask the teachers to discuss the practical issue of coping with pupils' different ability levels. In her response, each refers to her own classroom experience:

> I think, in *our* school, in *our* particular situation, streaming works. And I think it ... it's the best solution to our problem ... because ... I mean, I've taught under both – I did it when we had non-streaming – and when you had non-streaming it was ... *extremely* difficult to deal with ... It was *awful*.
> (Joanne)

> I can tell you where anybody in my class is on a book ... But, I feel I *have* to be doing that because, otherwise, you can't have children working individually.

> ... And so, when people say, 'Well, you can't deal with them individually',
> I think you *can* deal with them individually, but it's hard work, and it
> requires a lot of organization ... and so, that's what irritates me when I hear
> people saying – not bothering about meeting a child's individual needs –
> and, thinking of the sort of children *I've* taught ... if you can't meet the
> child's individual needs ... then, that child might as well not be at school.
> ... So, you've no *choice*, I don't think. You know ... to be effective you've *got*
> to meet individual needs – to meet individual needs you've got to be on the
> ball yourself. (Amanda)

If you were to base your selection on this information that Joanne
and Amanda have provided about themselves, whom would you
choose?

The comments presented above were actually made by two teachers, but not, of course, during job interviews. Joanne and Amanda are
both teachers who were employed at Rockville County Primary
School, and who participated in my research as interviewees. Their
comments tell us quite a lot about what kind of teacher each of them
is – at least, probably enough to allow us to form an initial impression
of which, of the two, we would prefer to appoint.

The basis of this initial impression – that is, the 'kind' of teacher
that each seems to be – is what I refer to in Chapter 2 as professionality. The distinction between Joanne and Amanda is one of
professionality orientation. This chapter introduces and explains the
notion of teacher professionality and examines some of the leadership and management issues associated with it: in particular, leading
and managing teachers who manifest 'extended' professionality.

What is professionality?

Professionality is not a widely-known term amongst educationists. It
appears to have been introduced over twenty years ago by Hoyle
(1975), who presented a continuum of teachers' professionality
ranging from 'extended' to 'restricted'. Professionality, as described
by Hoyle, is not the same as professionalism. Professionality refers to
the knowledge, skills and procedures which teachers use in their
work, whereas professionalism refers to status-related elements of an
occupation (Hoyle, 1975). Professionality essentially combines professional ideology, job-related values and vision. It reflects what the
individual believes education and teaching should involve, and
incorporates individuals' predispositions towards, and levels of,
reflectivity, rationality and, to some extent, intellectualism or, perhaps more precisely, intellectual curiosity. It influences perspectives.
Whilst professionalism principally relates to ways, or even codes, of
behaviour, professionality fundamentally relates more – though not
exclusively – to ways and levels of *thinking* that underpin behaviour. I

define professionality as *an ideologically-, attitudinally-, intellectually-and epistemologically-based stance, on the part of an individual, in relation to the practice of the profession to which s/he belongs, and which influences her/his professional practice.*

Hoyle (1975) illustrates the range of professionality typically manifested by teachers by describing two extremes: the 'restricted' professional and the 'extended' professional. 'Restricted' professionality is described as essentially reliant upon experience and intuition and guided by a narrow, classroom-based perspective which values that which is related to the day-to-day practicalities of teaching. 'Extended' professionality, at the other end of the continuum, carries a much wider vision of what education involves, values the theory underpinning pedagogy and generally adopts a much more reasoned and analytical approach to the job.

Based on the evidence provided by their comments on differentiation, it is reasonable to assume that Joanne and Amanda were quite distinct in relation to professionality, though, in relation to professionalism, they may conceivably have been very similar. Joanne's views suggest that she is likely to be located at the 'restricted' end of the continuum identified by Hoyle, whilst Amanda seems more likely to be an 'extended' professional.

To anyone who has either been a teacher or spent prolonged periods of time in schools interacting with teachers, the descriptions and characterizations of 'extended' and 'restricted' professionality ring true and are recognizable, even though the terminology may be unfamiliar. Teachers' professionality orientations, though, are seldom immediately obvious to others. Since they reflect values, views and ideologies they may not always be strikingly evident in the ways in which people teach, so they are not easy to observe. It is no easier to spot whether a teacher veers towards 'restricted' or 'extended' professionality than it is to spot her/his political affiliation, religious beliefs or views on abortion: these usually take time to detect. But through day-to-day interaction with colleagues, conversing with them, and becoming familiar with the ways in which they think about and approach their work, their professionality orientation is gradually revealed.

By this process teachers find themselves able to place most – if not all – of their colleagues along the continuum. By the same process I was eventually able to locate on the 'extended–restricted' professionality continuum all of the twenty primary school teachers whom I observed and interviewed throughout my research. These teachers represented a wide range of professionality orientations. It is important to emphasize that professionality is represented by gradations, not polarities. 'Extended' and 'restricted' professionalities represent the two extremes, but it is not a question of teachers having to be located at one or the other extreme: it does not follow that, if a teacher is not an 'extended' professional then s/he must, therefore, be a 'restricted' professional. There are degrees of 'extended'-oriented professionality and degrees of 'restricted'-oriented professionality. Teachers' location along the continuum is norm-referenced: it is determined in relation to, and by comparison with, other teachers. The two extremes are defined by exceptional atypicality.

The importance of professionality

Professionality orientation, as I point out in Chapter 2, is an important factor in relation to teachers' morale, job satisfaction and motivation levels. The reason why it is so important is that, because it reflects teachers' values, beliefs, ideologies and in many cases intellectuality, it determines what is their 'ideal' in relation to their work, which, in turn, influences their work-related goals and expectations. If teachers believe, for example, that teaching should have a rational, rather than an intuitive, basis – which is one of the characteristics that Hoyle (1975) identifies as distinguishing 'extended' from 'restricted' professionals – and if they find themselves working within a school professional climate that features much irrational decision-making and policy-formulation, then their job-related attitudes are likely to be adversely affected because their realistic expectations are not being met. Where there is congruence, on the other hand, between a teacher's professionality orientation and the professionality orientations of those of his/her colleagues who influence the school's professional climate and ways of working, s/he is more likely to experience job satisfaction and high morale. My research has revealed the degree of this kind of 'professionality match' to be a key determinant of teacher morale, job satisfaction and motivation levels.

In particular, although there were some exceptions, it was the more 'extended' professionals who were, for the most part, the most dissatisfied, demoralized and, in some cases, demotivated of all the teachers in my sample. To illustrate the nature and the extent of the 'professionality mismatch' that caused this, I present the cases of three teachers, employed at three different schools.

Mark, Helen and Amanda: Three 'extended' professionals

Amanda, Helen and Mark were all what I would categorize as 'extended' professionals. Their 'extended' professionality became apparent in the course of general work-related conversation with them. In the cases of Amanda and Mark, who taught at schools where I carried out observation, it was evident in classroom discussions and staff meetings, and in the ways in which they worked. In the cases of all three, their 'extended' professionality was evident in their comments made during research interviews. Mark's description of himself is illustrative:

> I believe passionately in ... good education, and having sound aims and objectives ... and, you know, having purpose to what you're doing. ... I don't mean to sound big-headed, but I do look for the rationale behind things and I do look at the theory and the philosophy. I like to read reports and documents.

In particular, each of them manifested an interest in undertaking further study and was either registered on, or seriously considering following, a higher degree or similar long award-bearing course. Indeed, participation in such courses is another of the characteristics identified by Hoyle (1975) as distinguishing 'extended' professionals from 'restricted' professionals, who typically prefer shorter courses of a practical nature.

Whilst all of those teachers whom I labelled 'extended' professionals manifested characteristics which were clearly oriented towards the 'extended' end of the continuum, they represented different degrees of 'extended' professionality. In the cases of Amanda, Helen and Mark, such a difference was apparent, but this did not preclude there being a striking similarity between the factors which they considered to have been significant in affecting their job-related attitudes, and the kinds of events and circumstances that shaped their separate stories, which are presented below.

Mark's story

At the time of his research interview Mark was 32 years old and had been teaching for six years. He had been at Leyburn County Primary School for the last four of those six years, where he was originally appointed as the science co-ordinator. He was a late entrant to the profession, having left school at the age of 16 with GCE O levels and, finding office work unchallenging, embarked upon a four-year Bachelor of Education (B.Ed.) Honours degree course at a local college of higher education, so that he could become a teacher.

Mark was, overall, dissatisfied with his job at Leyburn. He was not dissatisfied with teaching as a career. Indeed, he spoke of how he derived job fulfilment from working with children:

> I get a lot of satisfaction when children understand a topic I've covered. This year I've had a re-think on how to teach decimals ... and something as

> simple as that gives me a lot of satisfaction, when I've tested them and
> found that they could do it . . . and there've been quite a few experiences
> like that in the last couple of years, and I've got satisfaction out of it.

His dissatisfaction emanated from school-specific issues, in particular from what he perceived to be poor leadership. He made no
attempt to disguise his dislike of Mrs Hillman, the Leyburn headteacher, of whom he spoke very critically. He complained that her
highly efficient management presented a false image of a 'good'
school and obscured what he perceived to be the lack of sound
underlying educational principles and ideologies. He proceeded to
give an example of this superficiality:

> Mrs Hillman *knows* what the right things are in education. She knows that
> you have a class assembly . . . and combined topics . . . that you involve
> classes of different age ranges in activities . . . but, it's only superficial – it's
> not in the sense of . . . we get round the table and discuss, and say, 'Well, we
> need to do this – let's do something that's meaningful to you and the
> children.' . . . A few years ago she dropped on us a work experience . . .
> 'Schools' Involvement in Industry' . . . and she dropped on us the topic,
> 'The World at Work'. And we all had to set up a market place and do
> different topics related to industry. . . . But she just said, 'You're doing this',
> and everyone was totally bewildered, really . . . most people hadn't had a
> good training and they didn't know what she was talking about . . . so they
> just said, 'What shall *I* do?' and so, in the end, she was just *telling* them,
> 'You do this, this and this . . . '. But it wasn't meaningful, and it wasn't
> purposeful, and . . . no real benefit was gained by the children.

In particular, Mark condemned Mrs Hillman for perpetuating
Leyburn's underlying speciousness through her leadership style,
which involved an exceptionally high level of efficiency, but which
glossed over the surface and swept problems under the carpet, in
order to present a false image of a 'good' school.

For Mark, job fulfilment was tied up with translating sound pedagogy and educational principles into practice through school
management: 'I want to ultimately be in charge of a school where . . .
sound aims and goals and philosophy are thrashed out, through
discussion, and put into practice'.

He explained how, over several months, he had eventually come to
recognize this career path as the one which would be the most
satisfying for him:

> I think I've changed. I've gone through phases, at times, of wanting to leave
> teaching to be an academic . . . to go and do research . . . or to write
> children's books . . . and the most fulfilled I've ever felt in my life was when
> I was studying at college and writing essays. . . . Er . . . I had a word with the
> LEA adviser, and he said he thought it was fine doing an MA degree . . . and
> I still fancy the idea, for personal reasons, but I'm back in the groove of

wanting to get on ... as a deputy head, and become a headmaster, which I
didn't want to do before.

Mark's dissatisfaction at Leyburn resulted in his actively seeking a
new post – though, since he was only prepared to apply for posts
which constituted promotion, his career ambitions clearly also
played a part in his decision to leave. His frustration and dissatisfaction emanated from a sense of unfulfilment both at teaching in a
school which, despite outward appearances, operated on a func-
tional, rather than a rational, basis, and at being denied the
opportunity to exert any influence on changing this situation: 'I want
a position which gives me more clout and more power ... an
involvement in the management of the school ... to be an integral
part of the decision-making machinery – which I'm not'.

Mark's case was clearly one of mismatch between his own and his
headteacher's ideologies and values and between the different professionality orientations which they each represented. The headteacher's leadership style was such that her somewhat 'restricted'
professionality permeated the whole ethos and culture of the school,
making it unconducive to the kind of organization and practice
which reflected Mark's more 'extended' professionality. It was 'professionality clashes' of this kind which were similarly the underlying
causes of both Helen's and Amanda's dissatisfaction.

Helen's story

Helen was 42 at the time of her first research interview and had
worked as a teacher of early years children since leaving teacher
training college at the age of 21. When I first interviewed her she
held a mainscale teaching post with an incentive allowance B at
Woodleigh Lane Primary School, but was waiting to take up an
appointment in another school, Ethersall Grange Primary, giving
her an incentive allowance C. She had left college with a teacher's
certificate, gained an Open University degree through part-time
study and was working for an MA degree. For over a year she had held
a part-time (0.25) post at her local university, for which she was
seconded from her teaching post. Her university work involved
teaching on the one-year primary Post-Graduate Certificate of Education (PGCE) course on one-and-a-half days a week.

What distinguished Helen as an 'extended' professional was her
dependence upon extra sources of job fulfilment, beyond those
which were class teaching-based. She spoke of the job satisfaction
which her PGCE course teaching afforded her, and of how her
university-based work had prompted her to consider a career in
higher education:

> I think it was just, kind of, being around people at the University, and talking, and partly thinking, you know, 'Could this be the next chapter in my career – actually moving into this?' ... The way headship is now, that would be preferable to being a head. I think ... what I've got out of working at the University is a little bit of the things we've just been talking about – about working with staff. Because, I find that, certainly working with post-graduate students, has been like running INSET[1] ... but at a more basic level ... and I've found it exactly the same, because you can't just *tell* them things, and you can't just be didactic ... you actually have to set up situations where they can learn and come to conclusions for themselves ... But, I am finding that very satisfying ... working in that way.

Like Mark, Helen experienced much dissatisfaction and frustration in her job, which she attributed to poor management and leadership in her school. She spoke scathingly of her headteacher, complaining that he lacked vision and was ineffective, and that both the quality of education provided in the school and the prevailing professional climate had been greatly impoverished as a result of his inadequate leadership:

> In my opinion, not only has the school not moved on, but we've actually gone backwards! ... All the ... you know, the 'extended' professionals, are just going. ... There's nobody in that school with any vision – nobody with any educational philosophy – and that's what *really* frightens me to death. ... Because, they think that you just go in and you teach, therefore children will learn. They don't seem to realize what a curriculum really is.

However, despite her extreme dissatisfaction with her present situation, Helen's morale was high at the time of this first interview, since she anticipated much more opportunity for fulfilment in the new post to which she had been appointed, and to which she looked forward eagerly: 'I actually feel that I can be part, again, of moving a school on ... of actually developing and growing in all sorts of ways – all of us, together'. She spoke enthusiastically of the headteacher with whom she would be working at Ethersall Grange, and who had clearly made a favourable impression on Helen:

> My new school – my *next* school ... when I was in visiting last week they'd got the children's reports back from the head, and, where the teachers had written ... er ... say, four or five lines on the children's personal and social development, the head had written a good, sort of, five-inch column. ... And I flicked through a few, and it was different for every child. She knew each child, and she knew what she was writing ... And that immediately inspired me. I thought, 'This is somebody I want to be allied with.' ... I just *knew* – I like the whole way she is with people ... she's got a real vision ... a real educational philosophy.

Helen was one of those teachers whom (see Appendix) I interviewed twice, with over a year's interval between interviews. Unfortunately, by the time of her follow-up interview Helen was again dissatisfied with her job, since her new appointment and, in particular, the school's headteacher, Julie, had failed to meet her high expectations:

> I get very frustrated seeing heads making a hash of things. And I know that sounds arrogant, because I know the job's ... awful, in lots of ways. ... But, I *am* disappointed – I'm *very* disappointed ... I am *very* disappointed. ... The sad thing is that ... that I guess she still has all that I thought she had ... vision ... a sound philosophy ... but ... she cannot put it into practice. ... She's been ill. She was appointed head about four or five years ago, and then, after she'd been in the post for just over a year, she had this ME, this ... viral fatigue. ... And I assumed that she was fully recovered, but I don't think she is. ... It puzzled me right from the start ... she seemed very ... 'odd' with me when I first went ... hardly spoke to me ... I was certainly expecting some kind of talk about ... you know, my role in the school, and the set-up of the school, and I got nothing – I had to pick it up as I went along. ... I've had about ... two ... bits of positive feedback since I've been there. So, it's just as bad as at the other place, really. ... So, yes, I *am* disappointed – I'm disappointed with the whole set-up.

More significantly, Helen's latest disappointment had the effect not only of creating dissatisfaction but of demotivating and demoralizing her and influencing her perspective on teaching as a career. She was now disillusioned to the extent that she had begun to doubt whether she would ever find job fulfilment of the kind that she had once experienced when working with a headteacher whom she had respected and admired. This demoralization had prompted her to re-consider her career path, and to re-define her 'ideal' job. At the time of her first research interview Helen had described her 'ideal' job as a headship, in which she would enjoy working with staff in order to provide children with the kinds of experiences which she would want them to have. She had referred to the possibility of embarking upon a career in higher education, but had identified this only as an option. A year later, she was much more committed to a career in higher education:

> My ideal, *now* is to be actually working at university or polytechnic level ... certainly, that's where I see the future. ... I'm afraid I've just reached the ... er ... you know, that stage ... I'm struggling to keep going what I want to do – what I think's important.
> *Interviewer. And how much of this is to do with the national curriculum, and how much is a result of school management?*
> Er ... it's hard to measure ... but my feeling is that *most* of it is to do with school management.

Helen had actually applied for a lecturing post at what was then a polytechnic college and, at the time of her second interview, was waiting to hear whether or not she had been short-listed. Her decision to escape from what she perceived as the relentless frustrations of working in schools which lacked purpose, by seeking a change of career, makes her case very similar to that of Amanda, the third of my dissatisfied 'extended' professionals.

Amanda's story

Amanda was a late entrant to the teaching profession. After leaving school at 18 with A levels she had worked in the Civil Service and then brought up a family before undertaking her training as a teacher, which she completed at the age of 31. Like Helen, Amanda was interviewed twice. At the time of her first research interview in 1989 she was employed at Rockville County Primary School, having been promoted since her appointment to what was then a scale 2 post with responsibility for developing the school's religious and multicultural education. She was, however, seconded on a full-time basis from her post in order to work at the local college of higher education. This seconded post involved both participation in a religious education curriculum evaluation project and teaching on the four-year B.Ed. course. The secondment to St Catherine's College was for one year, initially, with a probable extension to two years. Amanda had held her post at Rockville for four years and, at the time of her first interview, was in her thirteenth year as a teacher. Rockville was her second permanent post, to which she had transferred from South Street County Primary School, under the County's voluntary redeployment scheme.

Amanda was an extreme example of 'extended' professionality, who consistently applied such a high level of reflection and analysis to all aspects of her work, and whose apparent perspective on, and concept of, education was so incisive, that she was distinct even from other teachers whose professionality orientation lay clearly towards the 'extended' extreme. Her description of the thoughtfulness and thoroughness which she applied to planning her teaching conveys something of the meticulousness which permeated her practice:

> ... whatever I did in the classroom, I did it as if it – when I planned for something I planned for it ... some would say, 'Well, the last time I planned like that I did it for assessment'. ... Now that's how I planned for *everything* ... that's how I got my job satisfaction ... you have to keep very 'au fait' with what's available, and when something new is introduced into the school you've got to be able to appraise *that* and your supplementary material in the light of what's going to be mainstream. .... So, I suppose, in a way, a lot of my satisfaction is not coming directly from teacher-child contact ... it's coming from, I suppose, in *my* way, being as organized as I can ... being as aware of what's available as I can ... reading as much as I can ... and finding out as much as I can about how to meet individual needs *for* children, and putting a lot of time and effort into organizing my teaching activity to accommodate what I know is appropriate for those children.

Yet, as with my other 'extended' professionals, her perception of teaching went far beyond a narrow, classroom-bound focus. She saw teaching as a career which incorporated continued personal and professional development, underpinned by constant self-appraisal and self-improvement.

As a class teacher at Rockville, though, Amanda felt constrained by the school's management and by the prevailing collegial culture which, she felt, emanated from the attitudes of those in management roles and of her teaching colleagues. She spoke of her interest in teacher development, and of how her work in higher education had allowed her to pursue this interest, whilst constraints at Rockville had restricted the job fulfilment which she derived from her work there:

> The work I like at St Catherine's [HE College] is where I'm supporting somebody in ... er ... preparing for school practice ... my interest is in ... er ... developing the professional competence of teachers. I *did* get a lot of satisfaction from teaching the children ... I still would now, but it ... it's not enough for me. ... And, having gone to Rockville thinking that there was going to be a high level of interaction amongst my teaching colleagues, which was about professional expertise, increased competence, extending and developing your own ... er ... teaching performance ... er ... by examining the children's learning and seeing what it needed – your in-service being how you could enhance your teaching and, hopefully, the children's learning as well ... what I *found* was ... the image I'd been given wasn't real ... and so I still found myself in a situation there where, generally speaking ... I felt that ... er ... I lacked colleagues who saw it as a career or as a profession. ... And, so, what does one do about it? ... Well, I was fortunate, wasn't I, that the project at St Catherine's came up ... it allowed me to ... er ... I suppose, develop professionally outside of whatever restraint was being put on it either by the school – the attitude of those in management positions ... the expectations of those who were determining what was the 'norm' for those children there.

Amanda's extreme dissatisfaction with the general way in which Rockville was run clearly stemmed from professionality mismatch. Her ideologies and values were at odds with those reflected in the professional culture which prevailed in the school. Decisions at Rockville were based upon practical rather than educational or pedagogical considerations and were often strategically rather than ideologically motivated. This imposed constraints on Amanda, in so far as she was often thwarted in her attempts to apply a rational basis to her own teaching, and she was able to exert only limited influence on school policy and practice. More significantly, her realistic expectations of how the school would be run were not met. She was both disillusioned and unfulfilled. In her first interview she spoke of wanting to leave teaching:

> Yes, I do want 'out' now ... but, for why? It's not because I'm jaundiced in teaching ... it's because I don't honestly believe that I'm ever going to have the opportunity, unless I get a deputy headship as a step up to a headship, to actually *implement* what I believe to be sound educational practice, on account of ... er ... well, I suppose ... the philosophy of others.

Amanda's second research interview took place in 1992, three years after her first one. She had not returned to Rockville. The post to which she had been seconded allowed her to develop contacts through which she was recruited to a team of providers of in-service courses and consultancy. She also successfully completed a part-time MA degree course.

The valve of extended professionality

My research revealed evidence that 'extended' professionals like the three whose cases I have presented represent a minority. I do not imply, by any means, that most teachers are 'restricted' professionals, but, if my sample of teachers is representative of the profession as a whole, most of them fail to exhibit all of the professional character-istics that Mark, Helen and, in particular, Amanda, exhibited.

To some extent, my research findings suggest that those who manifest characteristics of 'extended' professionality are, to varying degrees, marginalized by their own educational philosophies and ideologies. They suggest, too, that the talents of 'extended' pro-fessionals are being wasted and that the value of such teachers remains largely unrecognized. Many teachers do not value educa-tional theory and research as bases upon which to develop classroom practice and school policy and organization. 'Extended' profession-als typically do value them. Mark's report of a discussion with an LEA adviser illustrates the underlying problem:

> But the thing that's decided for me whether to do an MA ... I was talking to the adviser and he said to be very careful because sometimes people who do an MA in primary education are regarded as ... as outcasts, in a way, because they're quite alienated. It's an unusual qualification and it's quite often – although it might be fulfilling – it's not really to do with actual practice. So, when it comes to interviews for promotion, he said that someone who'd done a Certificate in something, or a DASE[2] – and I feel a bit insulted that I've to do that, after getting a 2i for my degree! – is given more prestige than an MA, because it's related to classroom practice.

Other researchers – though they may not use the terms 'extended' and 'restricted' professionals – report similar findings. Elliott's (1991, p. 315) reference, for example, to 'reflective sub-cultures' which, he claims, 'can be found in pockets in many schools' illus-trates his view that 'extended' professionality exists on the fringes of staffroom culture. Similarly, Nias refers to the marginalization experienced by those of her graduate teacher interviewees who manifested professionality which lies at the 'extended' end of the continuum:

> One of my interviewees put it this way, 'I'm intellectually lonely at school, I'm the only one who reads the *Guardian*, the only one interested in politics or literature and there is only one other who's ready to talk about art and music'. Similar comments were: 'My educational reference group is certainly not in school – it's a few intimate friends from university and scientists generally.' ... 'I feel intellectually starved'. (Nias, 1989, p. 49)

The outcome of this marginalization, though, is that the talents of 'extended' professionals may often go to waste. Unlike many of their more 'restricted' professional colleagues, those of my sample who were 'extended' professionals were not content with being able to teach in their own classrooms in accordance with their own ideologies. They were dissatisfied, frustrated and often demoralized if wider school issues, policy and practice failed to conform to standards which they considered appropriate. Their job-related ideals reflected much wider visions than those of many of their colleagues, but this meant that their ideals were less likely to be met. Moreover, the frustration which resulted from this was exacerbated by their feelings of not being heard, of making little headway towards 'converting' colleagues or towards influencing their schools' prevailing professional climates. As Helen said, 'I feel like a voice crying in the wilderness'. The real danger, of course, is that individual schools, and the education system as a whole, lose out because they fail to appreciate the value of 'extended' professionality.

But, what do 'extended' professionals have to offer? Certainly, in the case of Amanda, although she did not appear to be appreciated, and was not utilized to her full potential, by the headteacher and other senior staff, her talents were recognized by several of her Rockville colleagues. This was evident in the complimentary, even slightly reverential, comments made about her. Brenda, for example, spoke of Amanda:

> I respect what she does as a professional *immensely* ... I mean, I think she's probably the most brilliant teacher that ever – she's probably the most dynamic ... the most energetic ... the most gifted – I think she *is*. I think she's fantastic! (Brenda, Rockville teacher)

Hilary, a specialist ESL teacher who taught at the Language Centre which was housed at Rockville, and who had worked extensively with Amanda, corroborated Brenda's evaluation:

> I've got a great deal of respect for Amanda ... in fact, I would love – I've learned a lot, working with her – and I would love to be a fly on the wall to

> see how she handles the difficult – in fact, she had the worst class in the
> school and she had them working! . . . She's everything that a teacher *should*
> be . . . she's got a way where she's not having to shout her head off all the
> time.

The Rockville school secretary, too, made reference to Amanda's
professional qualities, summing up with, 'Well, she's wasted at Rockville, isn't she?'

Wastage and undervaluing of 'extended' professionality does not
seem to be confined to the UK context. North American researchers
(for example, Hayes and Ross, 1989, and Veal *et al.*, 1989) have also
highlighted the impact which schools' professional climates may
have on teacher reflectivity. Hayes and Ross's (1989, p. 348) case
study of Jennifer, whom they identify as a reflective teacher, illustrates the detrimental effects of mismatch between teachers'
professionality and school climate: 'At Northside . . . Jennifer's experiences . . . created defensiveness, lowered self-esteem, extreme
dissatisfaction with teaching and, at times, acquiescence to practices
which violated her basic beliefs about teaching'. In contrast, they
describe her response to working in a climate which was more
conducive to 'extended' professionality:

> In this environment, Jennifer drew on educational literature to develop
> innovative practices, engaged in continuous self-assessment, and her pro-
> fessional self-confidence soared. In fact, she described her first year at
> Canter as exhilarating. Her principal shared her perspective, saying that
> she was one of the best kindergarten teachers he had ever seen.

This last quotation highlights the potential value of 'extended'
professionals and illustrates what, under the right circumstances and
in the right contexts, they are capable of achieving. The extent to
which they are allowed to fulfil their potential, though, is very much
determined by the headteacher or principal and, in secondary
schools, also by departmental or faculty heads, and the kind of
leadership that they exercise. If 'extended' professionals are to make
valuable contributions to their schools the headteacher and, ideally,
other senior teachers, must play a pivotal role in getting the best out
of them.

Getting the best out of 'extended' professionals: The role of school leaders

Throughout her research interviews, Amanda provided examples of
the ways in which the prevailing professional culture at Rockville
and the attitudes of the headteacher and his deputy constrained her
professional practice to the extent that she felt she was not able to

teach in the way that she would ideally have liked. In particular, she regretted being unable to meet children's individual learning needs to the extent to which she considered herself capable:

> Now ... er ... when I asked about parallel classes at Rockville, before I came there, I was told that they were ... er ... streamed, and that they were streamed according to language ability. Now ... I don't actually agree with that ... and I did say, at the time, that I didn't agree with it ... and I was asked why, and Geoff and Margaret listened to what I had to say ... and I didn't say it off the top of my head – I mean, I had ESL children in my class ... you know ... I had a mixed class at South Street ... er ... anyway, that was the way it was done. When I took account of the fact that there were 60 children in each year I could see that, whichever 30 you had, there was going to be a sufficient span ... so I asked them what happened about remedial help, and ... er ... if I was going to have a less able class, because there were going to be 30 ... and I was told it was small group work. Well, of course, that *never* realized ... and what became obvious was that, for the most part, the less able children were allowed to be less able ... and it was put down to either laziness, stupidity, or the fact that they weren't English mother tongue ... and yet I *knew*, because of all the language work I'd done, that, generally speaking, nearly *all* their needs could be met ... and I couldn't do it with 30 in the class. And I felt that I'd been very misled there ... *very* misled.

Amanda's 'extended' professionality and her ideological incompatibility with the Rockville professional culture were never more apparent than when she explained the reasons underlying her frustration and dissatisfaction. The comments that I quote above were continued:

> ... and *also* disillusioned by the fact that ... teaching colleagues appeared, other than with a bit of light-hearted grumbling, unwilling to take any action in support of similar instances. ... They had similar situations arising for *them*, which they were willing to grumble about but not do anything about. Now, we're not talking about who makes the tea in the office, or somebody's not taken the tea-towel home to wash this week – we're talking about behaviour which is influencing a child's education. Now, if the job's of any status it's of status because you've a child's education there. ... We're not there to solve one another's problems – we're there to teach the children, so that the children can learn. And it seemed to be more about them teaching and less about children learning. ... And there were so many other things happening ... which, to me, were contrary to the stated ethos of the school – you know ... if you can *state* what the ethos of a school is – well, certainly ... what was being stated didn't match what was happening. I found ... I mean ... I didn't like the racist and socially divisive views that were being expressed ... I'm not saying we all have to have the same political views – even the same ... er ... I don't think we all have to view society in the same way in a school ... but a school states – Rockville made statements about ... you know ... it valued the child ... it valued the home background ... but the conversations I heard were

entirely contrary to that. We talked of welcoming parents in, and people complained that parents *wouldn't* come in, and then spoke about parents in a derogatory way. There was no sympathy for the fact that the children were bridging a culture gap on behalf of the parents . . . there was no real valuing of what the child was bringing in with them. There was no real valuing of the child – children were seen as nice or pleasant – but, unless they fitted into the fairly stereotyped view of what a good child is . . . Westernized, middle-class . . . then, in actual fact . . . er . . . the child, in some instances, received . . . less education . . . you know . . . and I say that advisedly because, obviously, I would have to substantiate it – and I *can* substantiate it!

The potential that Amanda had for positively influencing the quality of education that Rockville provided is self-evident. Under the right managerial conditions – and gradually, over time, and employing tact – she could have taken a leading role in advising colleagues on ESL and special educational needs (SEN) teaching. She could have been given a platform for advising on home–school liaison. In the right position she could have helped turn the school around. But she did none of these things. She was stifled and impeded because the headteacher evidently failed to recognize her potential value. Not only was she not encouraged to disseminate her ideas, but she was, on several occasions, discouraged or even prevented from effecting school-wide policy and practice that she suggested either because, she was told, her ideas were contrary to established policy and practice, or because the deputy head opposed her ideas.

Another of my Rockville interviewees gave her views on the reasons why the headteacher failed to get the best out of Amanda:

Amanda questions development and the intellectual side of things . . . and that's the side Geoff can't handle. It's a much lower level of decision-making that goes on at management level – not *curriculum* development. . . . Amanda would consider content, children's needs, suitable assessment . . . and he doesn't want to know! He's not interested! . . . Amanda . . . she challenges his position too much, and he is inadequate to . . . he's inadequate because he's no sense of direction . . . he's in the wrong job . . . er . . . and, intellectually, he doesn't worry about – nothing worries him . . . he lacks depth in educational development – in the development that *should* be going on in the school . . . he's inadequate. (Hilary, ESL teacher)

It was not just Geoff Collins at Rockville who failed to derive the maximum benefit from a talented member of his staff. The other two 'extended' professionals whose cases I present in this chapter were constrained in similar ways to Amanda. Their headteachers failed to recognize their value, with the result that, in each case, the school did not benefit from their talents to the extent that it could have, and the 'extended' professional him/herself became demoralized and dissatisfied.

Analysis of my research findings led me to identify two main reasons why headteachers fail to get the best out of 'extended' professionals. First, their own professionality is so far removed from the 'extended' end of the continuum that they simply do not have the capacity to recognize – let alone appreciate – the value that 'extended' professionality offers. Under these circumstances 'extended' professionals are constrained as a result of ignorance. They are stifled by someone who, technically, is their professional 'superior', yet who, in reality, is intellectually inferior to them. This was the case with Helen's headteacher at Woodleigh Lane. Such headteachers, as I point out elsewhere (Evans, 1997b) represent a lower calibre of school leader than is acceptable, and which, hopefully, as a result of recent government initiatives for improving the quality of leadership in schools in the UK, is eventually likely to become increasingly atypical. It will, however, take several years for all the 'old guard' who are currently occupying headship roles to die out.

Second, headteachers may consider 'extended' professionals a threat to their leadership, or, perhaps more accurately, their credibility as leaders. 'Extended' professionals may even provoke feelings of inadequacy in such heads, who may consider it *their* role to be manifestly the most reflective, analytical, 'on-the-ball' member of staff. Their vulnerability and insecurity may lead to their feeling undermined by more 'extended' colleagues, and their reaction may be to effect an intellectual and professional power struggle. This reaction is understandable, but misguided.

I certainly believe that all schools ought to be led by heads who are 'extended' professionals. If they are not, there is a danger that policy- and decision-making will be intuitively rather than rationally based, and the education provided will be impoverished as a result. However, there are, as I have already pointed out, degrees of 'extended' professionality, and I do not consider it essential, by any means, for the headteacher to be the *most* 'extended' professional on the staff. The characteristics of 'extended' professionality, in my opinion, include a receptivity to new ideas, a readiness to listen to and learn from others, and a willingness to discuss differences and make reasoned, rather than prejudiced or unconsidered, responses. The headteacher who manifests these qualities will secure, and retain, the respect of all her/his colleagues, irrespective of whether or not s/he is the most highly qualified, the most knowledgeable, or the most intellectual amongst the staff. What is essential, as I suggest elsewhere (Evans, 1997c), is that the headteacher's professionality is sufficiently 'extended' to allow him/her to recognize the professional talents of other members of staff and to foster them, rather than stifle them. Headteachers must value, encourage and utilize 'extended' professionality in ways such as those identified by Brig-house and Woods (1999, p. 76):

> Earlier we noted some leaders' capacity to sweep away problems, not by minimizing them, still less by ignoring them, but mainly by turning them into opportunities for growth and development. Moreover, if they hadn't this gift themselves, they recognized its need and were good at identifying people in the organization who had it to a sufficiently greater or lesser extent. In short, if such leaders are not instinctively blessed themselves with the capacity, they recognize the need for such people and promote them to a place in the sun, both within their management team and, if they are perceptive about people, more widely within individual departments and in whole-school working parties and extra-curricular activities such as trips, drama, music and sport.

In contrast to most of the descriptions of headteachers that have appeared so far in this book, Rosenholtz (1991, pp. 64-6) refers to American school principals who evidently do value, encourage and utilize 'extended' professionality. Identifying as 'teacher leaders' those who 'revealed to others new ways of doing things', 'suggested and inspired ideas and discourse' and 'helped others with problems that seemed insolubly interlocked', Rosenholtz includes reference to the facilitatory roles of some of these teachers' principals. She quotes two teachers (p. 66): 'The principal gives me certain responsibilities. I developed and run a school committee for problems that come up. I help train new teachers.' 'My principal says I am one. He says I have to keep on my toes because people look up to me here. . . . Teachers come to me for advice and I'm more than willing to help'. 'Teacher leaders', as Rosenholtz (1991, p. 66) describes them, seem for the most part to be essentially what I would call 'extended' profession-als:

> Teacher leaders seem to position themselves on the cutting edge of the pedagogical frontier; they like to plunge, go for broke, boldly explore the realm of possibilities, and take action in the spirit of exigency rather than waiting for any problem to present itself. That feat, however, requires new and sudden insights, active learning, belief in a technical culture, and a long, successful practice.

The roles that these teachers have been permitted and sometimes, it seems, encouraged to take on are precisely the kinds of roles that would have utilized the talents of Mark, Helen and Amanda and allowed them to fulfil their potential.

Similarly, Wortman (1995, p. 21), an American school principal, describes what he calls 'my professional journey with one teacher':

> I knew from my frequent visits to her classroom that she had developed a strong writing program tied to a rich literature component. She was reluctant to share her expertise regarding writing because she was afraid

that she wasn't doing it well enough and that others could do it better. My goal was to help her develop confidence in sharing her knowledge and experience. Lohse was at first reluctant to host faculty meetings; yet, after several tries with my support, she became adept at running them. I also asked Lohse to present with me and with other teachers at various district and local workshops, nudging her even further professionally. . . . She now presents at state and national conferences, has been videotaped by the National Council of Teachers of Mathematics as an exemplary mathematics teacher, and is serving on a national committee that is influencing assessment practices in mathematics programs nationwide.

This enabling, mentoring-type role of headteachers is also recognized by Michael Ashford, the head of a Buckinghamshire primary school. He is quoted as describing the headship role:

> The role of a head of a big school like this is to train people for their future development. . . .
> I've always believed I needed to facilitate and enable people, but it's much more than that now. I get my satisfaction out of seeing others function effectively. . . . My role as I see it is as a facilitator and an enabler. (Pascal and Ribbins, 1998, pp. 67-8)

Exemplary leadership like this serves to inform a model for managing to motivate 'extended' professionals. The two quotations above illustrate two complementary ways in which headteachers and principals, as well as departmental and faculty heads, may value 'extended' professionality: first, by fostering it and second, by utilizing it. More specifically, school leaders may adopt the following approaches to promoting a culture of 'extended' professionality within their schools or departments:

- seeking evidence of the professionality orientation of job applicants, and appointing 'extended' professionals;
- promoting 'extended' professionals, where possible;
- recommending 'extended' professionals for Advanced Skills Teacher status;
- demonstrating approval by making examples of manifestations of 'extended' professionality – showing off and celebrating the work and achievements of 'extended' professionals to colleagues, school governors, parents, LEA advisers, district superintendents, trainee teachers, visitors;
- spotting the potential of teachers (often revealed through their contributions to discussions, their planning documentation and their teaching practice) and encouraging their development through:
  - ❏ encouraging and supporting advanced study and in-service education;

❑ allowing, encouraging and supporting experimentation, innovation and the generation of ideas;
❑ mentoring and advising;
❑ setting challenges;
❑ involvement in decision-making – regardless of age, status, and length of experience.

These approaches will foster a school/departmental professional culture in which 'extended' professionals will be enabled rather than constrained. Talbert and McLaughlin (1996, p. 132) point out:

> Departments, like schools, differ in the coherence of purpose or mission, norms of collegiality, and goals held for their students. Departments, even within the same school, vary in terms of expectations about teachers' classroom activities, critical examination of practice, and involvement in curriculum development. Some departments comprise strong learning communities for teachers where faculty meet on a regular basis to reflect upon practice, review student accomplishments, or share information about new strategies, resources or ideas.

By making sure that your school or department fits this description you will be managing in a way that motivates 'extended' professionals.

Notes

1 In-service education for teachers.
2 Diploma in Advanced Studies in Education.

CHAPTER 4

Speaking and listening: Giving teachers a voice

Introduction

In the UK one of the key features of education reforms over the last decade has been that of giving more people a say in what goes on in schools. Widening the constituency of schools' governing bodies and increasing their power has been the mechanism for extending participation in policy- and decision-making to the general public and to parents. The latter have also effectively been given more opportunities to make their views heard through schools' increased accountability to them, reflected by statutory reporting, the Parents' Charter and open enrolment.

Yet, although more people outside schools have been given opportunities for involvement in decision-making, there have been few such changes affecting those inside. Whilst the governing body may question, challenge and, conceivably, intervene in and alter the way a headteacher runs his/her school, no such rights are afforded the teachers who work there. Of course, many teachers may be perfectly comfortable communicating to school managers and leaders their opinions on how their schools are run: in some cases they may be invited by management personnel to do so. There are many schools in which an atmosphere of open and candid expression of views is cultivated. The key issue, though, is that these opinions may be taken into account, or they may be ignored. Representations of teachers' ideas and concerns are accepted or rejected at the discretion of the headteacher and, ultimately, the school governors.

It is not unreasonable to assume that teachers' job-related attitudes will be influenced by their perceptions of how much real say they have in the school-specific issues that affect their working lives. In preceding chapters my illustrations of specific situations and circumstances have touched upon consideration of the extent to which teachers consider their views to be taken into account by senior colleagues. This chapter expands upon the issue. It focuses more narrowly on examination of how morale, job satisfaction and motivation are affected by teachers' perceptions of the extent to which they are listened to, and their wishes considered, by those who make key decisions. It discusses some of the management implications of giving teachers a voice.

Taking account of teachers' views: Rhetoric or reality?

Many school leaders would claim that they *do* give teachers a voice – most of them would undoubtedly be very sincere in believing that they actually do take teachers' views into account. Of the ten primary headteachers interviewed by Pascal and Ribbins (1998), for example, the majority referred to what they considered to be their consultative leadership style:

> I try to explain my point of view. I hope I can compromise, if they persuade me their point of view is valid then I will move. (Interview with Sue Beeson, p. 82)

> I have also learnt over the years that whilst sometimes it is inconvenient to consult and it takes time, you can end up in a stronger position by finding out what people feel about particular issues. If you have actually been consultative and you have got everybody together and there is the professional agreement to go in particular directions, then you will get them working together and this allows you to achieve more in the long run. (Interview with Michael Gasper, p. 126)

> I do believe that six or seven minds are better than one in tackling problems. I like to think I listen more than I did sometimes, and I think a listening, democratic style of approach is the way to do it. (Interview with Sue Matthew, p. 142)

> I am not afraid to compromise if someone has a better idea and I don't get too hung up on my own ideas. However, there are times when I do say I don't want to do it that way. But more often than not, I am quite open to suggestions, and I would normally say to people in staff meetings, this is the way I think we should do it and if you have a better way tell me and we'll go for that. (Interview with Usha Sahni, p. 201)

From the teachers' perspective, though, the reality may not be quite the same as how it is portrayed – and, for the most part, believed to be – by the head. In some cases it may be vastly different. Rockville County Primary School was one such case. The headteacher considered himself to manage in a consultative way. Although my research was not focused upon the attitudes of headteachers, I nevertheless inevitably found myself, as I came and went around the

schools in which I carried out observation, striking up casual conversations with the headteachers. It was in the course of these
conversations that I was able to gather clues that would help me to
construct better portrayals of the heads than could be put together
by observation alone. In response to my questions or comments
during such conversations with Geoff Collins he invariably indicated
that he did consult with staff, solicited their opinions on many policy
issues, and welcomed their approaching him with ideas and concerns. The Rockville staff, though, presented an other-side-of-
the-coin assessment of this consultative approach. An overwhelm-
ingly consensual criticism of Geoff was that, though he often went
through the motions of listening to and sometimes even soliciting
teachers' views, he generally disregarded them. To many, this was a
major source of dissatisfaction and demotivation:

> If somebody told me I was going to be at Rockville for another five years I'd
> go into another job. . . . I just think . . . er . . . I'm probably more aware of the
> situation, now . . . and more . . . frustrated, really. . . . I feel that I ought to be
> able to have more influence on it than I obviously can . . . whereas . . . when
> you go into teaching at first, you know that you can't . . . but now I feel that
> I ought to be able to . . . but, I can't.
> *Interviewer: Do those in charge ever ask your opinion about anything . . . and take
> notice of it?*
> Oh, yes. They *ask*, but, no, they don't take any notice . . . because it's only a
> token gesture. (Susan, Rockville teacher)

> *Interviewer: If you have an opinion and you go to the head with it . . . does he listen,
> do you think?*
> I think he'd probably *listen* . . . I don't know whether he'd do anything
> about it. (Stephen, Rockville teacher)

> . . . overall, I think Geoff does what he wants – and I think staff are
> consulted as a matter of good manners. . . . He's very sincere at pretending.
> He'll listen, and you think he's taken in some of your points, but, in the
> end, he goes his own way. (Elaine, Rockville teacher)

> I think, now, that he [Geoff] tends to listen and then just do the *opposite* to
> what you want. . . . I sometimes wonder if he listens to find out what – I
> don't know . . . I don't know if it's a deliberate action, or not – I mean . . . we
> come out of staff appraisal interviews – and we *all* feel like this – I mean . . .
> you tell him what you think in these staff interviews, and . . . we got just the
> *opposite* of what we'd asked for! (Pat, Rockville teacher)

Indeed, in many cases, it was consultation that Rockville teachers
highlighted as a key issue that detrimentally affected their working
lives and which was a significant attitudes-influencing factor:

> *Interviewer: What changes would you make in the school . . . the things that 'get' to
> you – how would you rectify them?*

Susan: More consultation . . .

Jean: Well, *proper* consultation . . .

Susan: Yes, *proper* consultation . . .

Jean: Geoff would say he *does* consult everyone.

Susan: Well, he *does*, yes, but he doesn't hear what you say.

(Susan and Jean, Rockville teachers)

> I still think he [Geoff] does a lot of things wrongly, and I tell him so to his face . . . er . . . I mean, I've never held back on my punches that way, you know . . . I mean, I've told him . . . er . . . his basic fault is that he doesn't talk to his staff . . . he talks to everybody else about what he's going to do – he talks to the advisers and the governors . . . and every Tom, Dick and Harry . . . but he doesn't talk to his staff. (Joanne, Rockville teacher)

There are different ways in which school management may have the effect of disregarding teachers' views. These different ways reflect the school's predominant professional culture. They are influenced by the personalities and, to a large extent, professionality orientation of key personnel as well as by the quality of professional relationships. The Rockville head was approachable and teachers were clearly comfortable raising issues with him and, for the most part, voicing their concerns. Their views were largely ignored, though, because the head was very much a 'restricted' professional whose vision was narrow and who did not consider it necessary for policy and practice to be underpinned by a rationality that reflected awareness of educational issues. Geoff Collins' rationality was more strategically and intuitively than ideologically determined. Teachers' views were also ignored not only because they emanated from non-senior staff and because they conflicted with those of senior teachers, but also because they conflicted with Geoff's own views and threatened to disrupt the plans that he had formulated prior to consultation.

In some schools teachers may not have a say in what goes on because the prevailing professional culture reflects a more authoritarian regime. In these contexts there may not be mechanisms in place within the management structure for allowing consultation. Even if they are in place, they are often likely, in reality, to be tokenistic since teachers may often – depending on their personalities – feel too intimidated to speak out. Some of the headteachers of whom my interviewees spoke seemed, to varying degrees, to have adopted these more authoritarian approaches to management, but with the result of provoking generally negative attitudes amongst their staff:

> I was reading a document about four weeks ago . . . and it said that the type of school that looks efficient is one where the head dictates and talks . . . and there's no coming back to the head – no feedback. I mean, our school,

it's just . . . Mrs Hillman *says*, and there might be one or two things fed back, but there's no interaction – no communication. There's no, sort of, coming to a decision by consensus. (Mark, Leyburn teacher)

And she *isn't* actually good with people. She goes through the *motions* of being good with people, but, in actual fact, she's quite autocratic. . . . And, although she comes across as being quite democratic, she actually isn't. People can't make decisions, because she will override them. (Helen, Ethersall Grange)

Now, you wouldn't think she's a dominating person, but she is, really . . . er . . . she makes it *appear* very democratic . . . and that we all have a say . . . but, when you sit back, after a staff meeting . . . who's won? Well, it's always Mrs Hillman . . . and that's because no one really voices an opinion or voices what they really, really feel . . . because she has a way of being very scornful . . . I've seen her do it with the deputy head a lot, and I just wonder whether it's *that*, at staff meetings . . . whether you *don't* say anything in case you get that . . . that scornful tone she can sometimes put on . . . and belittle you – I mean, she *can* do it – she can make you look – and feel – very small. (Ann, Leyburn teacher)

Evidence of non-consultative school management is not confined to my own research findings. In the context of the secondary sector in the UK, Ball (1987, pp. 109-13) describes teachers' reluctance to speak their minds when their views are at odds with those of their authoritarian heads:

> A history teacher at a southern comprehensive describes his head:
> > If it's a suspect area, if the head thinks there might be some opposition, he will make quite clear what his opinion is on it, so if anybody is going to say anything, they've got to appear to be going against the headmaster. . . . And there are only three of us who are willing to say anything and it would all be very reasonable. But I do it less than I used to, because I felt it was just counter-productive. It wasn't getting us anywhere, and you were considered as the token radical on the staff and you would have your say and they would say right the next person and you are ignored really. (Ball, 1987, pp. 109-10)

Rosenholtz's (1991) study of the different contexts in which teachers work identifies distinctions between what she refers to as collaborative, moderately isolated, and isolated schools. Autocratic leadership was found to be one of the features of those schools that she categorized as isolated, and whose teachers she quotes (p. 57):

> When there's a problem, if you don't totally agree with the principal's decision, you're labelled as a rebel, and accused of not trying to fit in, of being a trouble-maker. He labels us. He thinks we are a threat. I think he is intimidated. He makes you very hesitant to make a comment. There is a lot of retaliation by the principal.

His viewpoint is too authoritarian. He has to be above the teachers in all instances. He won't allow input into solving a problem; he doesn't value input from teachers. He is mainly dictatorial. He will try and figure out the problem himself, and then he will tell us what to do.

In a broadly similar study of schools' professional cultures in the UK Nias *et al.* (1989, pp. 149-50) found examples of decision-making processes that, even if they were not necessarily intentionally so, were effectively non-consultative as a result of teachers' reluctance to question or challenge headteachers' authority: 'Teachers and ancillaries generally accepted, or came to accept, their heads' authority, even when it was not exerted in an openly assertive fashion'. They illustrate the nature of this authoritarianism-by-default:

As for sitting down at a full staff meeting and chewing over the concept of doing an integrated day, I don't think those of us who were there when Mr Handley came would have dared say that we didn't like it. We got the feeling that this was going to be done and we jolly well had got to try and make it work. And let's face it, if a head says it will, it will, and that's the way it's done, isn't it? (Teacher, Hutton)

If it really came to it in the end – making a decision between their views and mine and we'd really thoroughly discussed it – they would in the end say, 'Yes, we'll do it your way because you're the head'. Because although they're very strong, I think that underneath they have got a respect that I'm the head and it's as simple as that. (Head, Lowmeadow)

The research evidence that I have so far presented illustrates teachers' dissatisfaction with school leadership that, one way or another, disregards their ideas, opinions and concerns. However, this is an incomplete picture. There is some research evidence of leadership that allows teachers to have some influence on the running of their schools. In my own study there were two very different examples of this. The first example is that of Woodleigh Lane, which is the school where Helen (see Chapter 3) was employed at the time of her first research interview. Here, an extreme example of a *laissez-faire* headteacher, according to Helen, allowed her and her colleagues considerable input into what went on in the school because he was, in Helen's words, incapable of making decisions: 'Decisions are *not* made. I'd even prefer it if decisions were made that turned out to be wrong. I can't stand indecisiveness'. Helen's quotation at the beginning of Chapter 2 provides some indication of the degree of freedom that she considered herself to have in this school: indeed, she refers to her own 'autonomy'.

The second example is that of the leadership of Sefton Road Primary School, in which I carried out observation. Although Phil, the headteacher, sometimes operated a rather unsystematic and spasmodic approach to consultation, most of the Sefton Road staff felt that if they had an idea to suggest, an issue to raise, or a concern to express, he would give it serious consideration and make a reasoned response. In this sense, Phil was perceived predominantly as an enabling leader:

> If you come up with an idea and say, 'I'd like to try this', and you can justify it and it sounds pretty good, then he'll back you. . . . I think he does like to see you trying out new ideas . . . not just jumping on the bandwagon, but . . . like . . . saying, 'Well, I think this would be a good thing to do'. . . . He'd very rarely stop you from trying out something that you wanted to have a bash at . . . as long as it fitted in with the school . . . he does *listen* to what people have to say. (Kay, Sefton Road teacher)

Similar evidence is provided by Nias *et al.* (1989, p. 70). In their study of primary school staff relationships they identified consultative leadership and shared decision-making as features of what they categorize as 'cultures of collaboration' within schools:

> The free exchange of work-related information and ideas contributed both to the professional development of the whole staff and to its social cohesion, that is, it simultaneously built up the team and developed the group:
>
>> In other schools I've worked in there would be talk, but it would be more general in nature, of what you were all doing in your spare time, whereas there's an awful lot of professional talk here. I did find it very strange at first, not having been used to it. To be expected to contribute an idea or articulate what you've had an intuition about is very different because not every head expects his staff to have a view. Obviously this is a school where they like you to have ideas, which is rather nice. (Teacher, Greenfields)

The evidence that I have presented suggests that teachers want to be consulted and to be seriously listened to. Is consultative leadership therefore the way to get the best out of people? Does involving staff fully in decision-making motivate them? The issue is not quite as simple and straightforward as it initially appears.

What motivates teachers?

Teachers, like anyone else, are motivated by what gives them satisfaction. They are much more willing to undertake fulfilling than unfulfilling, pleasurable than unpleasurable, or enjoyable than unenjoyable activities. Quite simply, then, if teachers find participating in school policy-formulation and decision-making enjoyable or fulfilling, they are likely to be motivated to undertake these activities and satisfied if they are given opportunities to undertake them. So, is consultative management – real consultative management that does more than simply pay lip service to consultation – a motivator? To answer that question I refer to more research findings.

There is evidence that teachers do not necessarily welcome being involved in school policy- and decision-making. In what he describes as an ethnographic style case study, Hayes (1996) examined the effects of one headteacher's attempts to develop collaborative decision-making in her school. The research findings revealed diverse attitudes amongst the staff towards participation in the initiative:

> Mrs Boxer [the headteacher] assumed that teachers would wish to participate. However, it was clear from their responses in the formal meetings that some teachers were more enthusiastic or confident than others about participation, and subsequent interviews with teachers indicated that assumptions about their involvement were presumptuous. Teachers spoke of 'making choices' about where to put their efforts and, when time was short, considered it part of their professional responsibility to concentrate more on matters that affected their classroom practice and their ability to relate to children throughout the school … than involvement in broader school management activities. (Hayes, 1996, pp. 293-4)

Hayes' interpretation of what he refers to as 'the varied and complex patterns of staff responses' (p. 291) is that they were influenced by teachers' ideals- and goal-focused priorities: 'It was hard to avoid the impression that for many teachers collaboration was only viewed positively when it facilitated the promotion of their ideals' (p. 295); 'the need for personal gratification from school-teaching did not allow the majority of staff to accede to propositions or decisions that they perceived as restricting them from achieving that goal'(p. 297). This corroborates my interpretations (see Chapter 1) of morale and job satisfaction: that they are essentially individual rather than group phenomena and that they are fundamentally influenced by individuals' proximity to their job-related 'ideal', which determines their goals. Clearly, then, participation in collaborative decision-making is fulfilling to some teachers, because it takes them nearer to their 'ideal-self-at-work', but not to others, whose 'ideal' may be more classroom-focused. Professionality orientation is likely to be reflected in this diversity of attitudes, but so, too, is level of involvement in the job.

Teachers do not all share the same levels of commitment to their job. For some, it is a major part of their lives; they may devote many hours of what might otherwise be leisure time to work-related tasks, the job is extremely important to them, and they afford it extensive consideration and high priority. Others may perceive it differently. To them, teaching is just a job, rather than one of the most significant features of their lives. They may carry out their duties conscientiously, and they may enjoy the work, but it is not their 'centre of gravity' (Goodson, 1991, p. 35).

Vroom (1964, p. 144) describes this commitment-level factor as 'ego involvement' in one's job. Goodson (1991, p. 42) refers to 'definitions of ... professional locations and of ... career direction'. Lortie (1975, p. 89) labels it engagement: 'People differ in their readiness to involve themselves in work; to some it is a major engagement; to others, something less'. His study, involving interviews with nearly 100 American teachers, included examination of the relationship between engagement and work satisfaction. His sample represented a wide range of engagement with teaching, from those for whom the job was evidently a major preoccupation: ' ... one heard statements like "teaching is my life". Such teachers connected travel and other activities to their classroom work; teaching was definitely the master role which organized other aspects of their life', to those described as 'relatively passive, with low commitment ... their interest in work was low' (Lortie, 1975, pp. 93-4).

If teaching is afforded relatively low salience the decisions made and the policies that are implemented are, for the most part, likely to matter less to teachers than if the job were given high priority. The comments of one of my own teacher interviewees illustrate this:

> I think teaching is ... I mean, I *enjoy* the job – I like doing it ... I really do ... but ... to be perfectly honest ... it's not my *life* ... and, therefore, the things that happen aren't *crucial* ... whereas, they would be to other people, perhaps. (Brenda, Rockville teacher)

For the most part, the teachers involved in my own study manifested concern to be listened to, to feel that their views and opinions were taken seriously, and to be able to have a say in the running of their schools. In some cases – particularly those of more 'restricted' professionals, or those teachers whose level of engagement in their work was quite low – it was often only in matters that impacted directly upon their own teaching and other aspects of their working lives that they wanted to be involved. In other cases, teachers' interests were much more widely spread, and many teachers – particularly the more 'extended' professionals – wanted to influence school-wide policy-formulation and decision-making. Headteachers whose management tended to be genuinely consultative were therefore generally successful at securing high levels of job satisfaction, morale and motivation among those who valued opportunities to be heard. Phil, at Sefton Road, was such a headteacher. Conversely, 'extended' professionals were demotivated by and dissatisfied with school leadership that disregarded their views and ideas and limited their decisional participation. It was his exclusion from his school's decision-making process that prompted Mark's decision to leave Leyburn (see Chapter 3). Not all teachers shared Mark's level of concern to influence decision-making; some were quite content for, and indeed some even expected, their headteachers and other senior colleagues to make most decisions. This is consistent with Belasco and Alutto's (1975) findings that, although participation in decision-making is a central issue for teachers, they vary in the extent to which they want it. What most teachers did want, though, was the assurance that if they wanted to be heard and taken seriously, they would be. Essentially, then, in relation to being heard, what motivates one teacher does not necessarily motivate another. The headteacher or principal, or departmental or faculty head who wants to develop a professional climate that is intended to foster high levels of morale, motivation and job satisfaction, as widely as possible, must accommodate teacher diversity.

Managing to motivate: Giving teachers a voice

How, then, can school leaders manage their schools, departments or teams in ways that accommodate teachers' diverse attitudes towards shared decision-making? What is needed, ideally, is some way of allowing those who want a share in the management to have it, and those who wish to, to take a back seat.

The traditional way of managing secondary schools in the UK has been through senior management teams (SMTs) which typically comprise the head and deputy headteachers and, in some cases, departmental heads or other senior teachers. Since the 1988 Education Reform Act transformed the nature of the primary headship role, increasing its administrative responsibilities, SMTs have also been introduced in many primary schools. As Webb and Vulliamy (1996, p. 303) point out, although they were almost exclusively confined to the secondary sector before 1988, they are now a widely accepted feature of primary schools. Indeed, based upon the findings of their survey of 150 headteachers of large primary schools in the UK, Wallace and Huckman (1996, p. 312) suggest that 'the notion of team approaches to management has taken a firm hold in the primary sector, in large institutions at least'.

SMTs, though, do not, by any means, necessarily provide the managerial mechanisms for giving all teachers – or, at least, all who want one – a voice. Indeed, by definition they are divisive – separating those who make decisions from those who do not. This was particularly evident at Rockville County Primary School, the only one of the schools in which I carried out observation that had, at that time, a formal SMT. A widespread feeling of divisiveness was evident amongst my interviewees: colleagues were perceived either as managers or as the managed, reflecting Ball's (1987, p. 103) observation about SMT members, 'They come to be identified as "the hierarchy"; they are not seen as primarily a part of the teaching staff'. Many Rockville teachers expressed dissatisfaction with the decision-making processes in the school:

> *Interviewer. Could you, sort of, go through the sources of frustration that you experience at Rockville – however small or large. . . . Could you try to identify them?*
>
> Management . . . the sort of hierarchical structure that there is . . . er . . . the way that some people's opinions are taken into account more than others' . . . well, they're treated as . . . just as if they're better than other people and that their opinions are always the ones that matter . . .
>
> *Interviewer. Are you prepared to say who?*
>
> Alison . . . Margaret . . . Joanne and Rosemary . . . He [Geoff] has a management team, doesn't he? . . . without who he can't make any decisions at all – but that doesn't involve everybody. . . . I've been *asked* about things . . . but they never take note. (Susan, Rockville teacher)
>
> He's very proud of his management team! . . . It certainly doesn't involve everybody . . . no . . . 'cos we're not allowed to say anything . . . I just tell him, I say, 'Don't ask me anything, Geoff, 'cos nobody takes any notice of what I say!' (Jean, Rockville teacher)

Second, a sense of exclusion was added to that of divisiveness in the cases of all except two recently appointed teachers. Some teachers spoke generally about being excluded from the decision-making process and some gave specific examples of their views being disregarded, or their suggestions ignored. This reflects Ball's (1987, p. 103) observation: ' . . . those staff who are not part of the senior management team tend to think of themselves as excluded from the important aspects of decision-making. This is now a specialist function'. The policy of streaming children into higher and lower ability classes within each year group was criticized by several Rockville teachers. It was considered to be unsound on pedagogical grounds, and those whose educational ideologies were child-centred in orientation regarded it as an outdated, teacher-centred organizational strategy which was supported by the influential 'old guard' who constituted the SMT. Dissatisfaction arose amongst the staff when their request to the headteacher, Geoff, to consider abandoning the streaming policy was denied by the management team. Several interviewees expressed their disapproval of this decision. The following comments are illustrative:

> I think the children would benefit if they were unstreamed. But Geoff will *not* unstream . . . he mentioned it to Joanne and Joanne said, 'No way!', so the subject was never mentioned again. (Pat, Rockville teacher)

We asked for non-streaming ... but ... and the only people who want streaming are Joanne, Rosemary, Alison and Margaret ... I think he's [Geoff's] frightened of the ones that run the school, you know. I think he's frightened of what they'd say if he decided to change anything. (Jean, Rockville teacher)

I believe it is extremely difficult to effect meaningful consultation through an SMT approach to school management. The most enlightened SMTs will incorporate consultative processes into their decision-making. This is likely to involve, for example, presenting ideas and suggested policy decisions at full or departmental staff meetings, and/or each SMT member's soliciting individuals' views directly, or delegating this responsibility to others. Yet, even operating in fairly democratic ways such as these, the very existence of an SMT precludes a system whereby all those who want to have a say have an equal chance of being heard – and taken notice of. This is because SMTs are hierarchical. As their name implies, they are teams of *senior* members of staff. One of the implicit assumptions upon which this hierarchism is predicated is that those holding the most senior posts are the best qualified to make decisions: in other words, that seniority equates to decision-making competence. This may not, of course, be the case.

Hierarchically-based decision-making is exclusive. It respects seniority and status, affording them consideration over alternative, sometimes competing, claims of suitability for participation in decision-making. It overlooks recognition of the value and potential of those who are placed at the base of the hierarchy. It neglects consideration and utilization of individuality and fitness for purpose. It is myopically selective, it wastes talent and, in doing so, is susceptible to the engenderment of feelings of unfulfilment and resentment, as we have seen in the research evidence presented in this chapter. Day *et al.* (1998, p. 14) suggest that hierarchical management can result in those located at the lower levels of the hierarchy experiencing feelings such as 'a sense of inadequacy; inability to express oneself; inability to influence anyone; feelings of being shut out; increase in cynicism ... feeling that new ideas can only come from the top; and feeling that there is no way to communicate with those at the top'. Although it may be fairly efficient in terms of getting through an enormous managerial workload, hierarchical decision-making is not the best way to manage if you want to motivate as many members of staff as possible. As a school leader you therefore have to weigh up the advantages and disadvantages of managing hierarchically and managing democratically, and decide what your priorities are. I do not pretend this is an easy choice.

Since this book is about motivational leadership I will present some ideas for decision-making processes that are aimed at motivating as many members of staff as possible to 'give of their best'. Although I describe them as institution-level processes they may just as easily be applied on a smaller scale to the management of teams or departments.

A heterarchical, rather than hierarchical, approach to managing primary schools is suggested by Day *et al.* (1998, p. 11), who clearly share my view that change is needed: 'The time has come to consider radical alternatives to the traditional model. The phrase "the headship collective" is used to describe one such model.' This model is described (pp. 12-13):

> The management activity of staff is driven by the school development plan for that particular year, and each member of staff joins a number of temporary teams to carry out the task work specified in the plan.
>
> Instead of conceiving of the management task of the school as a series of functions to be supervised, it is useful to see it as a series of tasks to be undertaken within a specific time period. ... Once a programme of projects and tasks is produced, small teams could then be set up to manage them. By this method, individual management responsibilities would be for specific management tasks and for active membership of temporary task teams. Once a project is completed the team disbands.
>
> Some tasks in a typical school development plan may be quite short-lived, perhaps occupying a small team for a week or two. Others may be more substantial, ranging over a whole academic year and involving some change of membership as the project develops. Through the regular pattern of staff meetings, teams refer to the staff as a whole, making periodic reports and receiving recommendations, observations, responses and suggestions.

Among the benefits that the authors suggest are to be accrued from this structure are: the involvement of all staff in key management and leadership activities; the removal of frustrations often experienced when decision-making is attempted in too large a group; and an increase in enjoyment and commitment (Day *et al.*, 1998, p. 13).

It is important to remember, however, that to put pressure on reluctant teachers to share decision-making is as likely to create dissatisfaction as does excluding those who want more involvement. What is needed is an approach to managing schools which acknowledges and respects the diversity of teachers' individual job-related needs and which imposes constraints on as few people as possible.

Retaining the head's ultimate authoritative role, but reducing the risk of this authority developing into autocracy, by flattening out the hierarchy, dispensing with the deputy headship role, and putting into place in schools a committee structure for decision-making is one idea which could be pursued. The committee approach to management would be applied to all except day-to-day working decisions, which would be the responsibility of the headteacher or his/her proxy – or, in larger schools, proxies – who may be nominated as such, depending on the size of the school, on a yearly, termly or even weekly basis. Committees would be specific to areas of school organization and effectiveness, such as teaching quality, curriculum development, finance, and professional development. They could vary in their degree of specificity, or even incorporate more specific sub-committees. A curriculum development committee might, for example, incorporate curriculum subject-specific sub-committees. Teachers could select the extent and the level of their participation. Some may wish to sit on many, or even all, of the committees, some may wish to sit on none. This would be acceptable, but their subsequent criticism of decisions made would then be considered unreasonable.

The level of teacher participation in their school's committee system of management would determine the extent and the nature of the hierarchism which evolved as a result. But this would be a self-imposed hierarchism which would be within teachers' powers to change, and they would therefore be unreasonable to resent it. This certainly represents a sweeping change to school management and would need to be piloted before widespread adoption. It would perhaps need to be tested first in primary schools before its principles were incorporated in the management of large secondary schools. It is a management structure which is applied successfully to many university departments and, as a principle, seems potentially workable in schools. The biggest problem in implementing it is likely to be that of teachers having insufficient time, alongside all of their other commitments, to attend committee meetings. A potential solution to this would be to hold some committee meetings during the school day and relieve from teaching duties those who wished to attend. Dispensing with deputy heads – and, in large secondary schools, other senior teacher roles – would result in there being more 'non-senior' teachers available. Providing cover is therefore likely to be less problematic than under the current typical system of school management – although in secondary schools it would be a little more complicated by the need to match teachers' subject specialisms.

An alternative solution to the problem of time constraints would be to allow a limited number of staff members to change their roles, responsibilities and job descriptions – for a specified period of from one to three years – from those of teacher to 'teacher-administrator' or 'teacher-manager', allowing them to devote a proportion of their time to managerial-related work. This might result, for example, in their spending two-thirds of their time teaching and one-third on school management. To ensure that these 'teacher-managers' do not simply replace deputy heads or middle managers, it would be important to ensure that the committee structure allows – from amongst those who want it – as many other teachers as possible a share in decision-making. Or perhaps 'teacher-managers' could be elected on the basis of their willingness and suitability to represent, as far as possible, their colleagues' views. This structure would provide no fewer opportunities than does the traditional structure for teachers' professional development and paths for promotion to headships, through experience as committee members, chairs of committees, headteacher proxies and 'teacher-managers'.

A less radical alternative to this committee system of management is a more democratic and inclusive version of the SMT-type approach. This would involve one main decision-making committee but, depending on the practicalities involved, either it would be open to all members of staff who wanted to sit on it, or it would include representatives of non-senior teachers. It would also operate under open conditions, publicizing its agendas and issuing invitations for items to be submitted for inclusion in them and making available its minutes, as well as making provision for any teacher to attend any meeting in which s/he has an interest, or to submit her/his ideas and views for consideration by the committee.

If, as a school leader, the idea of operating an open committee management system is threatening to you, ask yourself why. Analyse the rationality and validity of your response. Two heads of large educational institutions to whom I put the idea of open management team meetings made very different responses. One, the principal of a further education (FE) college, said that he always tries to operate an open approach to decision-making since, on two occasions when he tried making decisions behind closed doors, keeping the process secret from the non-senior staff, the approach backfired on him and created more problems than had previously been in place – not the least of which was an erosion of trust and confidence in management. He responded to my idea by saying that, although his SMT did not include representatives of non-senior staff, I had certainly given him something to think about. He also said that he would not object to any member of his staff sitting in on SMT meetings.

The second head, an experienced headteacher of a large secondary school, was much less receptive to my idea of opening up the decision-making process by allowing non-senior staff access to meetings, 'Because,' he said, 'we might want to discuss something that we don't want them to hear'. This is a perfectly understandable initial reaction, but it needs examining. In order to examine it effectively, though, a change of attitude is needed on the part of school leaders to whom open decision-making poses a threat. If you fall into this category ask yourself:

- What am I afraid of?
- What is the worst scenario imaginable at an open management meeting?
- Is a management decision that is not generally supported by the staff a good decision? Who is going to benefit from it? Who will be disadvantaged by it?
- If, despite opposition, I believe my ideas are sound and worthwhile, what course of action should I adopt to get them implemented? Is imposing them on colleagues likely to be effective, or should I be trying to change people's attitudes?
- Does my role as 'leading professional' in the institution involve my fostering attitudinal development among staff? Do I have some responsibility for teachers' professional development? How might my promoting open discourse about policy and decisions contribute to this aspect of my role?
- Am I more likely to promote trust, collegiality and collaborativeness by being open and honest, or by being secretive and deceptive?

Then try to provide a sound argument to justify keeping the decision-making process closed.

The chances are that what deters you from opening up your decision-making process is fear of opposition, based upon a belief that some, or perhaps most, of your staff do not entirely share the values and ideologies that underpin your decisions. Winston (1992) describes such a situation, which faced him as a newly appointed primary school head. He wanted to adopt a consultative approach to formulating a management plan for his school but feared that one of the ideas for change that he wanted to include – promoting cross-curricular links – might be undermined by disapproval from teachers whose educational ideologies were, he suspected, more traditional in orientation:

> The fact that I feel driven to think in terms of alliances for decisions ... is an indication of the political struggle I see as an undercurrent in even the briefest of staff meetings. Eric and Martha, two of the more openly traditionalist members of staff, will use them as a platform to probe and reveal weaknesses in a way which I interpret as an expression of discontent with the values I represent as much as the desire for better organization or a wish to 'get at me' for personal reasons. The potential for a clash of values with the more established staff had been very much to the fore of my thinking. (Winston, 1992, p. 143)

Winston relates the process of applying what he describes as an ethically dubious strategy of manipulating a staff consultation exercise in order to ensure that his ideas for change were included into the school management plan. He reflects on this process, 'I was not ready to trust certain sections of the staff enough to bring them honestly into the decision-making process' (p. 144) and 'Far from emphasizing the collaboration and trust of the collegial model, my behaviour was politically motivated, with a significant body of the staff being identified as the ideological foe' (p. 146). He then describes, and reflects on his feelings associated with, the more enlightened approach he later adopted to raise the issue of the school's discipline policy at the next designated staff training day:

> It is difficult to think of a subject more capable of exposing the values and hence the potential for value conflict within an ideologically divided school. The fear and mistrust which underlay the working out of the school management plan earlier in the year could easily have led me to look for ways to avoid real discussion rather than promote it. . . . Over the summer, however . . . I had become more clearly aware of the contradictory pressures, both internal and external to myself and the school, which had distorted my practice, damaging its integrity and rendering it less consistent. Despite fears that I might find myself under ideological siege on the first day of the school year, I decided to risk making a deliberate attempt to encourage the mutual sharing of attitudes and values in an atmosphere of frank and open exchange. The day, carefully planned and focused, subsequently turned out to be very constructive. Everyone contributed and I felt we ended it as a more socially cohesive staff, with many underlying issues having at last been brought out into the open and an action plan reached through genuine agreement rather than acquiescence. (Winston, 1992, p. 147)

Perhaps this reflects realization and acceptance of some of the points made by Rosenholtz (1991, p. 63):

> Where principals reject teachers' ideas for school improvement, it is the threat of the very look it has, its veering from their control, its deviationism, that seems to be most feared. And as carriers of perniciousness, principals undermine teachers' participatory spirits, leaving them discouraged, defeated in spirit, and low in imaginative thought. Reality, teachers may then conclude, is that the nature of school life is completely intractable.
>
> It is clearly not the case, of course, that increasing teachers' involvement in decision-making represents a loss of principal control. On the contrary, it can be used to guide critical managerial decisions, helping principals to choose the most appropriate course of action, to select among multiple alternatives.

The benefits of shared decision-making to which Rosenholtz refers may be achieved by less radical means than I have suggested. Those who are considering branching out along this path – but in fear and trepidation – may wish to adopt the more gradual approach that they represent. A collaborative professional culture may be developed in any school – no matter how big it is – if those who manage it are committed to achieving it. Rosenholtz (1991, p. 44) reminds us:

> Norms of collaboration don't simply just happen. They do not spring spontaneously out of teachers' mutual respect and concern for each other. Rather, principals seem to structure them in the workplace by offering ongoing invitations for substantive decision-making and faculty intervention.

An example of the kind of 'structure in the workplace' to which Rosenholtz refers is provided in Wortman's (1995, p. 35) description of his school's collaborative and collegial processes. Some of the more distinctive features worth noting are:

> Staff meetings are held every Wednesday after school. The meeting rotates from classroom to classroom with each teacher taking responsibility for running the meeting. ... Any member of staff can request time on the agenda.
> ... Every staff meeting begins with people volunteering their joys or sorrows for the week. It's sometimes personal and sometimes professional.
> ... The host teacher shares some strategy or successful practice that worked well.
> ... The librarian always gets 5-10 minutes ... to introduce new books ... all books are checked out on the spot by staff. Everyone is responsible for knowing our resources, which are vital to making professional decisions.

Collaborative structures such as this are certainly commendable, and they represent a step – or several steps – in the right direction. The key issue, though, is whose views hold sway in the event of disagreement. Of course, people cannot expect to have their ideas adopted all the time. As a leader, there will be times when – for whatever reason – you decide not to follow a suggestion made by a member of staff; times when you decide not to meet a request, or accommodate a preference; times when you feel you have to say 'No'. What is absolutely critical, if you are concerned to avoid demotivating, is that you always offer a rational and honest explanation for a negative response. Giving teachers a voice is not about granting their every wish. But neither is it about simply going through the motions of consultation. As we have seen from the Rockville interviewees' comments, paying lip service to widening decisional participation is quickly detected and condemned by teachers, and it demotivates rather than motivates. Effective consultation and sharing of decision-making requires the right attitude in leaders – even if this means a change of attitude.

The right attitude involves acceptance – genuine acceptance, not nominal acceptance – that other people's views may be as valid as yours, and their ideas may be as good as – or better than – yours. The effective leader motivates by acknowledging this, and by manifesting open-mindedness and receptivity to alternative perspectives. It is this that constitutes giving teachers a voice.

CHAPTER 5

In praise of teachers: Motivating through recognition

Introduction

Giving teachers a voice is about affording them recognition – recognizing that their views and ideas are valid and worthy of serious consideration. This chapter continues with examination of the theme of recognition and expands it to incorporate consideration of the importance of recognizing teachers' efforts and achievements.

This aspect of recognition – recognition of the value of the work that they do – has become an important issue with teachers in most countries in the developed Western world. It is fundamental to subsidiary issues concerning teachers' working lives that have evolved or emerged during recent decades, such as the issues of lowered status in society and increasing deprofessionalization. In fact, so important an issue is deprofessionalization considered to be that it was the theme of the 1993 annual seminar of the Association of the Teacher Educators in Europe (ATEE).

In Chapter 1 I refer to the media's interpretation that teacher morale in the UK has been adversely affected by teachers' feelings of being undervalued, and, indeed, Doug McAvoy, the General Secretary of the National Union of Teachers, adopted this line in a public attack on the Chief Inspector of Schools:

> Chris Woodhead, the chief inspector of schools, fails to understand the impact he has on the morale and motivation of teachers, particularly at primary level. 'Half of schools failing their pupils' (*Independent*) and 'Kick out the teacher dunces' (*Daily Express*) were just two of the headlines emerging from the spin he put on the Ofsted annual report. ... Crude generalisations about widespread failure demoralise not the minority of poor teachers – they will by definition be fairly immune from external criticism – but the majority of effective teachers. (McAvoy, 1996)

In the context of the USA, McLaughlin *et al.* (1986, pp. 423-4) identify recognition as a key issue to emerge out of their research:

Lack of recognition was a recurring theme in our interviews with teachers. They told us that their work is difficult and important to the society but that – both from within the educational system and from outside it – they get the message that they are unimportant.

'In general, recognition [for one's work as a teacher] is so infrequent,' noted a dedicated teacher of high school English. 'Nobody says thank you,' declared another.

But what, if anything, can headteachers or principals do about this? Mercer and Evans (1991, pp. 297-8) point out that school leaders are limited in what they can do to increase the recognition afforded teachers by those outside the profession:

> How might the job satisfaction of teachers be increased? A major problem associated with tackling the problem at school level is that there are certain aspects of the teachers' lot which are not within the gift of the Head-teacher. We suggested earlier that one possible cause of job dissatisfaction was the teacher's feelings of worth as part of his or her self-image. To the extent that the teacher obtains feedback from the public, there is not a great deal the management can do about it. Although a Headteacher can raise the profile of a school locally, there is not much which can be done to improve the image of education nationally. Similarly, the teacher's feelings of worth as measured by pay is not a matter for the Headteacher to solve since this is essentially in the hands of central Government. Does this mean therefore that nothing can be done to improve job satisfaction at school level?

In fact, although they acknowledge that there are limitations to what can be done, Mercer and Evans do consider school leaders capable of reducing the damage done to teacher morale and job satisfaction by lack of recognition for teachers' work. They refer to school managers' failure to address the issue of job satisfaction amongst school staff as 'professional myopia':

> There appears to be an element of short-sightedness on the part of senior staff who have the responsibility for ensuring the highest quality of performance from teachers ... there is a great and perhaps largely unnecessary loss to the teaching profession. (Mercer and Evans, 1991, p. 297)

My research has demonstrated that there is, indeed, much that can be done within schools not only to buffer teachers against the demoralizing assessments of others, but also to make them feel appreciated for their efforts, and later in this chapter I present ideas for ways of doing so. First, I explain the rationale for avoiding this kind of 'professional myopia'.

The importance of recognition

Why is it so important to recognize teachers' efforts and achievements? Since they are adults and professionals, do they not carry on, day after day, giving of their best, irrespective of whether or not they are recognized for what they do? In order to address these questions and examine the importance of recognition we need to look at how it relates to job satisfaction and morale.

It is important to remember that this book is based upon what research has revealed to be influential upon teachers' attitudes to their work. In particular, it draws out the link between what gives teachers job satisfaction and high morale, and how this in turn motivates them. Analysis of my own research findings led me to formulate a model of the process whereby individuals – any individuals, not just teachers – attain job fulfilment. This model is represented in Figure 1.

I identify eight stages in the process of attaining job fulfilment, all of which, according to my interpretation of job fulfilment, are essential. These stages reflect the subjectivity of the individual experiencing job fulfilment and relate to her/his actions without necessarily reflecting general consensus and without necessarily incorporating objectivity. Below, I explain the job fulfilment process, stage by stage, as represented by my model.

Explaining the job fulfilment process

Stage 1

In the first stage the individual needs to be aware of an imperfect situation in relation to his/her job. What I mean by 'imperfect situation' is that there is some aspect of the job with which the individual – in the context of this book, the teacher – is not entirely happy. This may range from being a very slight 'imperfection' – something that is not quite as the teacher would ideally like it – to a major problem or difficulty. Like any other job, teaching involves dealing with many such 'imperfections' every day. In Chapter 2, for example, Amanda's reference to children in her class who were struggling with learning to read and who needed remedial programmes identifies what she considered to be an imperfect situation.

It is important to realize that it is the individual her/himself only who decides whether or not a situation is 'imperfect'. Other people need not share this view. For it to spark off the process of attaining job fulfilment, though, an 'imperfection' does not have to be obvious, nor does it have to be a serious or major deficiency. My interpretation of an imperfect situation, in the context of its being a

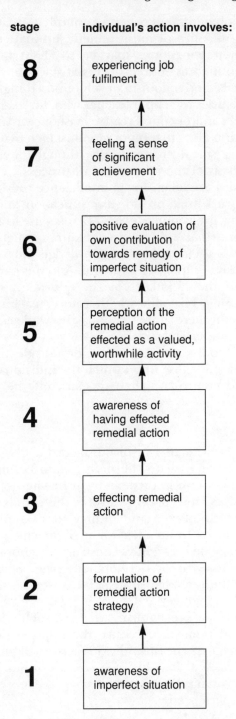

Figure 1   Model of the job fulfilment process in individuals

catalyst for the job fulfilment process, is simply a situation in relation to which some measure of improvement, no matter how small, is desirable. Such imperfections may be so slight that they would scarcely be identified as sources of dissatisfaction. Often they will reflect individuals' perfectionism or self-imposed high standards for themselves. The primary school teacher who, for example, feels that it is essential to hear every pupil read at least once a week will identify as an imperfection any situation or circumstance that prevents her/him from doing so. Most commonly, though, the imperfections which are the basis of the job fulfilment process are more general and pervasive and are taken for granted, since they represent constituents of the work itself, provide its justification, and determine its nature. Teaching, for example, exists as a response to an ever-present general situation – that children do not know enough. It is their not knowing enough – their inadequate knowledge and understanding – that is the pervasive 'imperfect' situation. And this particular 'imperfect' situation is the rationale for the education system and, of course, for teaching. Like all work, therefore, teaching is essentially about putting right these 'imperfections'. Its whole essence is that of a remedy to an 'imperfect' situation.

Imperfect situations may be within or outside the individual's control, but it is only those upon which the individual may exercise some degree of control which may spark off the job fulfilment process.

Stage 2
At Stage 2 the individual is involved in formulating a strategy for removing or reducing what s/he perceives to be imperfection, in order to bring about an improvement in his/her job-related situation. 'Strategies', as I interpret the term in this context, may range in magnitude. What counts as a strategy may, for example, be a passing thought which leads to an idea for a slight change to a way of working, or it may be a carefully constructed school improvement plan, or a personal career development plan. Stage 2 does not involve putting the remedial strategy into effect; it merely involves formulating it. It is a conceptual stage. It involves nothing more than the individual teacher's recognizing what s/he believes – even if s/he is wrong – would remove or reduce the imperfections. Remedial strategies do not have to be the individual's own original ideas nor do they have to represent her/his own creative input, but the more creativity and originality there is at this stage, the more job fulfilment is likely to be experienced.

Stage 3

This stage involves carrying out the remedial strategy. A successfully implemented remedial strategy points the individual towards the path which leads to job fulfilment. It is important to re-emphasize, however, the taken-for-granted element in the job fulfilment process, to which I have referred in my explanation of Stage 1. The implications of this are that the formulation and the putting into effect of what I refer to as remedial action or a remedial strategy need not necessarily be, and often are not, anything other than what is accepted and carried out as part of the work itself. Clearly, if imperfect situations constitute the rationale, and the very need, for the work, then, by the same token, the work itself *is*, in this sense, the remedial action. If, for example, pupils' inadequate knowledge is the pervasive imperfect situation which is the underlying rationale for schooling, then the job of teaching them is, in its entirety, the remedial action strategy. Thus, every time teachers teach they are actually carrying out, in a taken-for-granted way, remedial action in response to a prevailing imperfect situation. In this sense, it is the teacher's choice of teaching methods and classroom organizational strategies that are his/her remedial strategy. In other words, teachers choose to adopt a particular approach because they consider that approach to be the best way of reducing the 'imperfect' situation of children's inadequate knowledge.

Stage 4

Stage 4 occurs when the individual is aware of having effected remedial action. This awareness is essential to the job fulfilment process, yet it is by no means automatic that individuals who have formulated and effected a strategy for remedying an imperfect job-related situation will be aware of having done so. Since much of this occurs in the taken-for-granted way which I have described, by teachers' simply carrying out their day-to-day work which, in itself, constitutes remedial action, it may often go unrecognized by them. Teachers may not always be aware of the extent to which they have helped children, nor of the influence which they may have had upon their lives. Pupils' and students' responses to learning activities may be deceptive or misleading, resulting in even experienced teachers not only not overestimating, but even underestimating, their success. Unless there is an awareness of having successfully effected remedial action, job fulfilment – in relation to the remedial action in question – will not occur. Teachers cannot, for example, feel fulfilled because they have finally managed to 'reach' a problem child if they do not know that they have done so. One cannot experience fulfilment from something unless one is aware that it has happened.

Stage 5

This is a key stage in the process. It involves the individual's perceiving the remedial action which has been carried out as a valued, worthwhile activity. Without this perception job fulfilment, as I interpret it, will not occur. This perception is the key distinction between job fulfilment and job comfort (see Chapter 1). Job comfort may occur in relation to situations and events that individuals do not value particularly highly, or do not consider to be very worthwhile. They may, for example, experience positive job comfort if the staffroom is nicely decorated and has facilities such as a refrigerator or dishwasher – but they are unlikely to derive fulfilment from these facilities because they do not value them highly enough. The extent to which a specific activity has the potential to fulfil, rather than merely to be considered satisfactory, is determined by the status, significance and value attached to it by the individual. The higher the status and value afforded by an individual to an activity – and it is the individual's perception only that matters – the greater will be its potential as a source of job fulfilment. Of course, individuals value different things. Some teachers may value and derive fulfilment from participation in curriculum development, policy-formulation and decision-making, while others rate class teaching much higher.

The reasons why individuals value or rank things differently are complex. Perceptions of value may be influenced by many factors, such as professional cultural norms and attitudes, the views of respected colleagues, and institutional ethos. They are also influenced by biographical factors and individuals' experiences. 'Extended' professionals are likely to value different things from 'restricted' professionals. The value afforded by individuals to specific tasks or components of work does not remain static. It is liable to fluctuate in response to individuals' changed, and changing, circumstances and situations in their lives. What we value about our work is likely to change as we progress through a career and achieve advancement. Promotion to a higher status job may alter our perceptions of what it is about our work that we value – particularly since promotion often widens work responsibilities and introduces us to different tasks. Thus, for example, a teacher who is promoted to a deputy headship or assistant principal's post may find that the value formerly afforded coordination of the school's mathematics teaching is displaced by the value attached to newly acquired managerial responsibilities. Similarly, individuals' non-work lives are also influential on this dynamic process. If you are experiencing serious domestic problems it is likely that what you formerly valued about your work suddenly takes on less significance in your life.

Stage 6

Stage 6 involves the individual's believing her/himself to have been responsible – in part or in full – for remedying the imperfect situation in question. Without this attribution of personal success job fulfilment cannot occur. It is important to emphasize that, in order to attain job fulfilment, it is not necessary to consider oneself to have achieved *total* success in relation to carrying out the remedial strategy. Depending upon factors such as the standards set for her/himself by the individual (that is, how much of a perfectionist s/he is), and the circumstances surrounding each case, only a small measure of perceived success may be necessary in order to proceed along the path that leads to job fulfilment.

Of course, how much success in remedying the 'imperfect' situation individuals believe themselves to have achieved may be influenced by, or based entirely upon, the views of others whom they recognize as competent assessors of their performance. These may be headteachers or principals, heads of department, other colleagues, LEA advisers or district superintendents. Recognition of this kind serves as an important reinforcer of positive self-assessment. It is, however, important to emphasize that, whilst the views of others may be influential, they are not essential to individuals' self-assessments. Consistent with the focus on individuals' subjectivity which is reflected in all stages of the job fulfilment process outlined in my model, Stage 6 represents the individual's own, subjective, positive evaluation of her/his contribution towards the remedy of what s/he perceives as an imperfect situation. Precisely how this positive evaluation is formulated is unimportant. It is likely to be strengthened if the individual knows it to be supported by others, but, essentially, it reflects the individual's view only, even if this may be generally considered to be misguided. In the job fulfilment process, misperceptions at Stage 6 are as valid as what may be considered to be more objectively accurate perceptions. The teacher who holds firm to the view that s/he is the best teacher in the school remains well on track for experiencing job fulfilment even though colleagues, parents and pupils consider her/him to be the worst teacher they have ever encountered.

Stage 7

In most cases, Stage 7 is an inevitable stage which occurs automatically as a result of the previous six stages having been achieved. In some cases, however, the job fulfilment process is arrested once Stage 6 has been reached, because there are some circumstances which prevent the individual's feeling a sense of significant achievement, despite the awareness of having made an effective contribution in relation to a valued component of his/her job.

One of the factors underlying individuals' failure to feel a sense of significant achievement in their work is the relativity factor, which concerns the relative consideration which the individual affords to his/her work, or to aspects of it, alongside other competing priorities. Essentially, what this means is that, although it may be valued by the individual within the sphere of his/her working life, the job component to which s/he considers her/himself to have made an effective contribution is not valued enough, because work itself, in relation to other aspects of the individual's life, is not ranked sufficiently highly. Brenda, for example, whom I describe in Chapter 2 as manifesting quite a low level of engagement with her job – who prioritizes her work much lower than do many of my other interviewees – is unlikely to feel the same sense of significant achievement in relation to her work as are teachers who prioritize the job much higher.

Stage 8

Stage 8 is the final stage in the process: that involving the individual's experiencing job fulfilment, as I define it in Chapter 1. As my definition makes clear, individuals' job fulfilment does not necessarily apply to their work in its entirety, but may be specific to certain components of it, or even, within these job components, to specific activities and/or tasks. Teachers may be fulfilled by their interaction with children, for example, but not with the administrative tasks that they have to complete. More specifically, they may find fulfilment in teaching English – because it is their area of expertise – but not in teaching science, which they find difficult. Overall job fulfilment depends upon what is effectively an unconsciously-applied equation, or calculation, which balances fulfilling activities against those which are not fulfilling, at any one point of time, and which incorporates consideration of other, non-work-related circumstances and situations, bringing in the relativity factor. So, when a teacher says, 'I get fulfilment from my work', s/he is likely to be saying, in reality – and perhaps without being conscious of doing so – 'I have calculated that I get fulfilment out of interaction with children and seeing them progress, and I get fulfilment out of contributing my ideas for school policy-making, and from liaising with colleagues from other schools when I attend meetings of the district ... but I don't get any fulfilment at all from handling difficult parents, nor from marking essays, and I sometimes – but not always – get fulfilment from preparing form assemblies and seeing them go well ... so, on balance, because, quantitatively speaking, I get more fulfilment than "non-fulfilment", I can say that I find my work fulfilling'.

The role of recognition in the job fulfilment process

Once we understand the process whereby individuals achieve job fulfilment the part in the process played by recognition becomes clear. Although attaining job fulfilment is a subjective process that is determined by the perceptions, views and values of only the individual concerned, it is easy to see how these may be influenced by other people. In particular, recognition of teachers' efforts and achievements has the potential to make a significant contribution at Stages 4, 5, 6 and 7 of the job fulfilment process as I describe it.

The form of recognition that works – that is, that facilitates progress through the job fulfilment process – is positive feedback on their work from people whose judgement teachers value and respect. These people are most likely to be colleagues. Research has shown that feedback from senior colleagues – particularly those to whom teachers are directly answerable – is one of the most potent motivators. Praise from headteachers or principals, or departmental or faculty heads, motivates teachers to give of their best because – whether they realize it or not – it increases their chances of feeling the sense of significant achievement that is essential to achieving job fulfilment. Unlike Herzberg (1968) (see Chapter 1) I do not consider recognition for achievement to be a direct source of job fulfilment. As my model of the job fulfilment process indicates, I acknowledge only one fundamental source of job fulfilment – a sense of significant achievement in relation to what is perceived as a valued, worthwhile activity. However, I do accept that recognition is an important contributor to this fundamental source of fulfilment. It serves to confirm the individual's sense of achievement – to help persuade the individual that s/he has not made a mistake in believing her/himself to have achieved something. In some cases, it may serve as a confidence booster and raise self-esteem, contradicting the individual's perception that s/he is not doing a good enough job. Recognition for their efforts and achievements in the form of positive feedback acts as a strong tailwind that helps to push individuals along the job fulfilment process and encourages them to sustain – or even to increase – their efforts, in order to continue achieving fulfilment.

The importance of positive feedback is highlighted by those who have carried out research relating to teachers' job-related attitudes. Lortie (1975, p. 149) writes of his teacher interviewees, 'they crave reassurance which, for them, could only come from superordinates and teaching peers', and McLaughlin *et al.* (1986, p. 425) focus on the benefits of recognizing teachers' efforts and achievements:

> Our efforts to construct a workplace that will promote the effectiveness and

satisfaction of teachers should also include serious consideration of the nature and extent of feedback that teachers receive about their perform-ance in the classroom. The teachers in our sample said that their performance suffers because they lack routine, constructive feedback. Collegial feedback could help teachers solve recurrent problems and reduce their uncertainty about whether or not they are attaining their instructional goals.

Increasing the quality and the quantity of feedback to teachers achieves several goals. First, teachers broaden their repertoire of instructional strategies, which increases their effectiveness. Second, the investment of district resources in this enterprise sends a clear signal to teachers that their work has worth. Third, good teachers receive the recognition that is often lacking. Fourth, effective performance is maintained and burnout is avoided.

Rosenholtz (1991, p. 43) explains how feedback reduces the uncer-tainties that are so much a part of teaching:

> Where goals are ambiguous, where socialization and evaluation lend no clear direction, and where there is no common sense of purpose, teachers feel uncertain about a technical culture and their own instructional prac-tice ... but in schools where teachers receive clear performance feedback on mutual goals, they may suffer far less instructional uncertainty.

Positive feedback, she suggests (p. 107), allows teachers to 'gain some on-the-job estimate of their particular competence and worth'.

Evidence of the motivational potential of positive feedback is provided by Nias (1989) in her study of 99 graduate primary school teachers in the UK. Reporting what her interviewees had said about the importance upon their working lives of collegiality, she high-lights the particular significance attributed to recognition:

> But the interpersonal attribute both most valued and most noticeable for its absence was a readiness to give praise and recognition. Much was expected in this respect of heads. A man commented:
> > The head's a tremendous force in the school ... she can be a real demon and sometimes the tension gets you down because you know she's watching you all the time, but you really feel pleased when she pats you on the back.
> A woman in her first deputy headship said:
> > The head says he's pleased with what I've done so far and that's given me the confidence that I'm on the right track. (Nias, 1989, p. 146)

> Seven people spoke of the satisfaction they received from being praised or appreciated by colleagues or superiors (e.g. 'I like being told I've done something well. On the whole I do this job well, so I get plenty of praise. Maybe I wouldn't like teaching so much if people didn't tell me I was good at it'). (Nias, 1989, p. 88)

Yet, research has revealed that feedback is sadly lacking in most teachers' working lives. Rosenholtz (1991, p. 107), for example, concludes from her study of American teachers' working lives:

> Most teachers and principals become so professionally estranged in their workplace isolation that they neglect each other. They do not often compliment, support, and acknowledge each other's positive efforts. Indeed, strong norms of self-reliance may even evoke adversive reactions to a teacher's successful performance.

Similarly, referring to her study, Nias (1989, p. 147) writes:

> Unfortunately, headteachers were often found wanting in this respect. One teacher with fifteen years' experience explained that she had left her previous school because of the head's apparent indifference to her professional practice: 'He never once in six years asked what I was doing, came into my classroom or commented on anything he saw'. . . . 'The one thing I couldn't stand at [that school] was the head's lack of interest. It drove several of us out in the end'; 'The head didn't give you any feedback . . . I suppose in her way she was pleased with things that were going on and she recognized people's abilities, but she'd never ever let on and tell you'.

Ball (1987, p. 161) includes reference to similar complaints. He quotes a secondary school departmental head: 'The head won't provide what the staff are crying out for – paternalism. He never comes round the lessons and says you are doing a good job', and Lortie's American teacher interviewees (1975, p. 149) told the same tale:

> That teachers spend most of their working hours outside the view of other adults has consequences for monitoring their results. Some wish there were witnesses who could help in their self-assessment:
>
> > I don't have anyone to criticize me. Like my principal, sometimes I wish she'd give me a compliment or a word or two on how I am accomplishing something. . . .
> >
> > Lots of times you wonder. The principal never comes to see you or you never see some of the other teachers and you wonder, well, what do they think of you – are you doing a good job?

My own research revealed that recognition of teachers' efforts and achievements, through praise, was perhaps the most effective motivator. Teachers who were given positive feedback on their work by their headteachers reported higher levels of job satisfaction, morale and motivation than those who were not. Recognition of this kind, when it was merited, was a key feature of the Sefton Road headteacher's management. Phil would make a point of conveying to teachers his satisfaction with their work. He would compliment them on their latest wall displays, and on their plans for particularly interesting activities, which they had written about in their weekly record books. He would comment favourably on the progress that they were making with specific children, of which he became aware as he went in and out of classes, monitoring the work in his school. In this respect, his management style seems similar to that of John, a headteacher with whom Ann, from Leyburn, once worked:

> Well, at one school, Littlefield, we had a head who was a very good motivator and was very free with his praise . . . and he would come into your room and say, 'Oh, it looks lovely in here; oh, you *are* working hard!' . . . It was the praise business . . . *and* he worked hard himself . . . you knew where you stood with him. . . . But . . . er . . . he was a good motivator, and I think it was just that one little word of thanks every now and again that did it.

Phil, the Sefton Road head, lavished favour, in the form of personal attention and explicit approval, on those whom he identified as competent teachers. He would visit their classrooms to observe what was going on and to provide positive feedback. Those teachers with whom Phil was unimpressed were usually treated cordially, but received no such personal attention. His leadership style incorporated blatant favouritism, based on his perception and recognition of professional competence. I certainly do not suggest that this constitutes exemplary leadership, but what resulted from it was a school professional climate characterized by a competitive collegiality, which, in the cases of many teachers, seems to have been directed towards securing, or to have been sustained by, Phil's approval. In this sense he managed to motivate a large proportion of the Sefton Road staff.

Attributing it to Phil's influence, Sarah spoke of how this good-natured, friendly rivalry spurred on many of the Sefton Road teachers to greater effort and hard work:

> It's like an undercurrent. . . . He [Phil] doesn't *say* it . . . but he doesn't *realize*, I don't think, just exactly how much is expected of you . . . But he doesn't think it comes from him, though . . . because he was discussing with me once – I was saying that it's a hard school to work in – because he was saying he was finding it hard to find staff – quality . . . and he said that people outside perceive it to be a hard school, and I said, 'Well, it *is*', and he said, 'But, why? What is it that makes it hard?' and I said, 'Well, it's the standard to work to'. . . . But *he* said that he didn't think it came from him, and I said, 'Well, it comes from . . . everybody's gee-ing each other up all the time'. But we also work to his expectations. But he didn't realize that – he thought it was *us* that were making ourselves work hard. (Sarah, Sefton Road teacher)

The Sefton Road climate suited Sarah. She fitted in well at the school and, though she found the pressure to meet the high standards of expected performance a source of stress at times, she was content to stay there. It was clear that school-specific factors were very influential on her job-related attitudes. She referred to the good staff relations at Sefton Road:

> Now, the thing about here, as well, is that when you go into the staffroom you don't usually hear anybody griping about anybody else ... and everybody goes in and sits down and gets on ... we are fairly easy going.

But it was her relationship with the head that essentially underpinned her day-to-day job satisfaction and motivation levels. It was attention from Phil, in the form of recognition and praise, that seemed to be a very important driving force behind Sarah's positive attitude towards working at Sefton Road:

> I think I really do seek the approval of other people. ... I try to overcome it, but I think I ... I *need* praise and I need criticism ... and I'm not very good at taking criticism ... but I still need it. That's one reason why I left my last school because ... I could've got on with what I was doing all day long and, no matter what I put in, I didn't get, 'Oh, that's good', or anything. ... I didn't get any criticism, either. I got nothing ... and I was doing a heck of a lot there. I mean, I hate to think of it being like that, but I feel like I'm one of the children. ... I really do try to praise the children, and I always think of myself – how *I* feel – and I need encouragement. ... Phil gives us a hundred times more encouragement than my last head did ... and it ... because the staff is so big it's hard ... but I still need it all the time ... I *need* it.
>
> *Interviewer: Which is more important, praise from colleagues or praise from Phil?*
> Oh, it's got to be Phil. But I also feel good if John [the deputy head] says something ... because John is so good, and you think, 'Gosh, if *John* says that ...'. ... I would say that I wouldn't be as motivated anywhere else ... I don't think there'd be anywhere where I'd feel like this.
>
> *Interviewer: Is it Phil who's motivating you? Do you do it, sort of, to please him?*
> Er ... I would say that's probably true ... but I would also say that you see so much going on elsewhere in school and you're lifted by that.

Many of my teacher interviewees, however, who received no praise or indeed feedback of any kind from their headteachers, were dissatisfied and had become demotivated and demoralized by their efforts remaining unrecognized. Helen's analysis of precisely why she was dissatisfied with her headteacher's management and leadership focused on this issue:

> He's never set me any challenges, and he's never once noticed what I've done. And I've never once had any feedback. And I said to him, in one of my really bad moments: 'I could be teaching them Swahili, hanging by their heels from the light fittings, and *you* wouldn't know!' ...
>
> I *think* it was the lack of recognition that really bothered me ... that, whether I do it or don't do it, he doesn't think any different of me. ... I think it's that. ... As I say, in my classroom, he's never once come and said, 'Oh, that looks a good piece of work you've done with the children'.

Similarly, Fiona's, Ann's and Mark's comments about Mrs Hillman, the Leyburn head, highlight how detrimental had been the effect upon their job-related attitudes of her neglect of recognition of teachers' efforts:

She once said to someone, 'You never tell staff how well they've done ... because it makes them stop trying'. Now, to motivate people, you give them feedback ... and it makes them drive on. (Mark)

Fiona's leaving because of *her*, yes ... it's *totally* because of Mrs Hillman. She lost Mrs Earnshaw – a very conscientious ... er ... hardworking person ... because she wanted something doing *yesterday* ... and when it was done you always felt that it wasn't done as well as she would've liked it to have been done ... er ... she *never* gives praise! ... Er ... this is one of the first rules of teaching kids ... and we all like a bit of praise ... and she never, ever, gives praise. ... You never know quite where you are with her – or whether she likes you – or whether she thinks you've done a good job. (Ann)

She doesn't stand there and look, but she knows everything that's going on, and she can recall and sometimes throw it back to you ... or make a comment about something ... but, if it's favourable, it should be done at the time, and if it *isn't*, then, likewise, it should be done at the time ... but we never knew whether we were doing the right thing. ... I just no longer want to work for her ... it's just the fact that she'd never *say* ... she'd never say ... you got no feedback. I mean, if somebody's not doing the job properly, you should have them in your room and tell them – but there's not even *that*.
*Interviewer: Do you **need** feedback from the boss?*
Yes, definitely!
Interviewer: And Mrs Hillman doesn't provide it?
No. (Fiona)

Clearly, then, teachers are motivated by positive feedback from their headteachers or principals and also, in many cases, from other – particularly senior – colleagues. School leaders, though, are often unaware of precisely how much impact upon teachers' attitudes to their work they potentially have. Of those referred to in this chapter, most of the headteachers or principals who reportedly do not provide feedback to staff would probably be extremely shocked to discover that their behaviour is capable of demoralizing teachers to the extent of prompting them to seek other posts.

If you fall into the category of school leaders who seldom – or never – give praise, this chapter has probably been an eye-opener and, if you are concerned to get the best out of teachers, you clearly need to reassess how you manage the staff for whom you are responsible. Whether you are such a leader, or whether you already consider yourself to be successful in recognizing teachers' efforts and achievements, the next section – based on what research has found to be successful – will give you ideas for increasing your motivational capacity.

Managing to motivate: Recognizing teachers' efforts and achievements

Recognition may take several forms. It may be applied collectively, to the whole staff or to a whole department as a single unit, such as when a headteacher or principal, deputy head or head of department thanks teachers, on every appropriate occasion, for their efforts. This was one of the features identified by Nias *et al.* (1989, p. 105) of schools in which there existed what they refer to as a 'culture of collaboration':

> All three collaborative schools were characterized by positive reinforcement. It was clear that the heads put much faith in praise as a strategy for developing a supportive climate which built up teachers' and other staff's confidence and self-esteem. Staff were almost always welcomed, thanked and praised either directly or by reference to the children's work or behaviour.

This is certainly an effective form of recognition since it serves as a continued reminder to staff that their commitment and conscientiousness are appreciated. However, its effectiveness is considerably increased if it is supplemented with recognition that is applied to individuals and small staff units. This is the form of recognition that underpinned Phil's generally successful, and motivational, leadership of the Sefton Road teachers. It is particularly effective because it is highly personal and because it incorporates an element of exclusivity throughout the time that it is conveyed. It singles out individuals for special attention at a particular point in time and, in doing so, gives them a psychological boost that stems from their feeling that they have excelled.

It is important to emphasize, though, that unless great care is taken, such a personalized, individualized form of recognition may degenerate into favouritism. This would clearly reduce its effectiveness since it would engender resentment amongst those teachers who were generally excluded from it, and, whilst those who were favoured would be likely to remain highly motivated, the overall effect would be to dilute the motivation levels of the staff as a whole. At Sefton Road Phil sometimes came perilously close to this disadvantageous form of leadership because, as I explain in the next chapter, he overlooked consideration of what I identify as a key feature of motivational leadership – what I call individualism.

Whether it is directed at the staff as a whole or at individuals, recognition may vary in the manner in which it is conveyed. It may be implicit, such as when a teacher's work is selected for more public display than is usual. Implicit recognition may be reflected in a school leader's choices of teachers to mentor trainee teachers. It may be reflected similarly in choices of classes to include in visitors' selective tours of the school. It may also be reflected in the allocation of responsibilities, or in choices of classes in which to place problem pupils. The teacher who, for example, is asked to take on as her/his tutor group a notoriously troublesome Year 10 form (14–15-year-olds) is probably being implicitly recognized for her/his competence at handling disruptive students. Implicit recognition, however, is generally inadequate at motivating teachers and at enhancing their work-related self-esteem, since it is susceptible to misinterpretation. Unless s/he is explicitly told that it is her/his professional competence that has prompted the decision to allocate her/him a badly-behaved tutor group, the teacher in question may, for example, interpret the decision as a subtle ploy to drive her/him out of the school.

Explicit recognition, on the other hand, leaves teachers in no doubt about how their work is rated by others. The motivational school leader conveys positive feedback in many different ways, and on various occasions: through supportive written comments in teachers' planning books; through a spontaneous congratulatory remark after witnessing a teacher's success with a child, or after watching a well-presented class or form assembly, or on receiving notification of a teacher's excellent examination results; through an exclamation of appreciation on noticing an attractive classroom display, or a voluntary extra playground duty; or through a special personalized message of thanks in a Christmas card, e.g. 'thank you for all your hard work this term – and particularly for the time you've spent reorganizing the reading resources'.

Since research has shown that, in general, teachers receive insufficient praise from senior colleagues it is reasonable to assume that many school leaders fail to recognize just how important a motivator it is. There are several possible reasons for their oversight. It may stem from one or more of the following viewpoints:

- teachers, since they are adults, are not reliant upon praise to work to the best of their ability (this misconception may occur in school leaders who are, themselves, self-motivated);
- teachers, as professionals, *should* not be reliant upon praise as a motivator (this kind of attitude is typically represented by sentiments such as: Well, I shouldn't have to thank them, or praise them, for something that they're getting paid to do!);
- praising teachers may make them complacent – better to withhold it or use it sparingly to keep them on their toes.

Some school leaders, of course, may simply not be 'praisers': praising is not part of their nature. They may, themselves, have been brought up in an environment where praise was seldom given and so use of praise tends not to feature as part of their repertoire of social skills: they do not expect praise themselves, and seldom pay compliments of any kind to anyone, including their families.

If school leaders are to get the best out of teachers, they need to adopt the right attitude to giving positive feedback – many already do so, but, as I have illustrated in this chapter, there is also much room for improvement. The 'right' attitude involves perceiving positive feedback as one of the key components of the school leader's role. All too often giving feedback is considered to be peripheral to what are perceived as the main leadership tasks, which are invariably administrative. It is tagged on as an 'extra' – sometimes almost an afterthought – to be fitted in, if there is time, after the important jobs have been done. Reflecting this attitude, many school leaders – particularly busy headteachers of large schools – will make remarks such as, 'Well, I'd like to be able to go round praising teachers more – I know it's something I *ought* to do – but I never seem to have the time. Administration takes up all my time'. A change of attitude is vital. If you think – and it is perfectly understandable that you do – that administrative work is more important than interpersonal work, just remind yourself of some of the comments (presented in this chapter) made by teachers who failed to get feedback on their work from their headteachers. Consider how many were so dissatisfied and demoralized that they were seeking new posts, and ask yourself whether or not – in the interests of retaining, and motivating, good teachers – you ought to be relegating recognition of teachers' work to a subsidiary leadership and management task.

The following tips may be useful to school leaders who want to get the best out of teachers:

- Cultivate in your school or department a professional culture of collegial feedback. Encourage staff to visit each other's classrooms, or share successes, triumphs and concerns. Celebrate ideas for, and reports of, good practice – including all aspects of the job, such as record-keeping, planning or organization of resources, as well as interaction with children.
- Extend this culture to include parents, school governors, and, where appropriate, pupils and students. Encourage them to commend teachers' work. You could begin, for example, by sending letters home to parents – or addressing them at an open day or parents' evening – indicating

that, as head of the school, or head of the English department, you want to know if they are particularly pleased about something that one of the teachers has done with their child. Bear in mind, though, that positive feedback is best sustained if it is a two-way process, so set the ball rolling by encouraging teachers to commend individual children's specific efforts and achievements to their parents.

- Only give praise where it is merited, otherwise you risk devaluing it. But base your decision about whether or not praise is merited upon the individual's circumstances and situation. You would not, for example, expect the same standard of work from a newly qualified teacher as from an experienced colleague.

- Pass on all secondary compliments and convey your pleasure at having received them, e.g: 'I was delighted to hear the educational psychologist saying what an excellent job you've done with Susan'.

- If it helps you, create a designated book for keeping records of your feedback to teachers. Here you will jot down your own feedback, if it is inconvenient to pass it on at the time when it occurs to you, as well as secondary compliments (e.g. Tues. 10th – Miss Smith – overheard excellent questioning on causes of Second World War). Such a record will also help to ensure that you avoid neglecting some individuals.

- If you find it easier, pass on some of your feedback in written form.

- Where appropriate, phone teachers at home (e.g. 'I wanted to tell you this now, because I didn't catch you at school and I won't see you again until after the Easter holiday, but I was outside the upper school hall this afternoon for a few minutes and I overhead your form assembly ... ', or, 'I am *so* pleased, I had to phone you immediately. I heard a few minutes ago that three of your students have qualified for ... ')

- Where teachers consistently excel in their work let them know that you notice this. Don't just mention it in passing when you happen to bump into them – although that would certainly give them a boost – call them into your room, sit them down and tell them, formally, how delighted you are with their exemplary work (give examples) and tell them that you will commend them to the governing body at the next meeting.

- If you run a large school encourage other senior teachers, such as heads of departments, to pass on to you information about teachers' work that you would want to praise. But be honest with teachers and tell them that you received the information second-hand – don't pretend that you noticed their work yourself; they will easily see through this and begin to mistrust you.

- Remember that it is often taken-for-granted things that teachers ought to be praised for, but which are most often overlooked – things which are part and parcel of their work. To avoid oversight, make a list of the kinds of things for which you could praise teachers (such as handling of pupils; classroom displays; written planning; a specific lesson) and, if necessary, use this as the basis for gathering information that will allow you to incorporate into your leadership a more systematic – but genuine – approach to giving feedback.

- If you want to know whether you are giving enough feedback, ask the staff. If you feel it will generate more honest responses, ask them to complete a short questionnaire – anonymously.

CHAPTER 6

A teacher-centred approach to school leadership

Introduction

By focusing on different ways in which teachers are likely to be motivated, earlier chapters in this book have contributed to building up a picture of the kinds of specific approaches to school leadership that manage to get the best out of staff. The picture so far built up is one of a leader who is aware that the teachers for whom s/he is responsible are individuals, who differ in relation to what satisfies or dissatisfies them. It is also one of a leader who recognizes the importance of giving teachers a voice and allowing those who wish to do so to participate in decision-making, who is fully supportive of those members of staff who manifest 'extended' professionality, and who appreciates the value of praise as a motivational tool.

A limitation of this picture, though, is its specificity. It may serve as a useful illustration of the kind of leadership approach that gets the best out of 'extended' professionals – but what about dealing with 'restricted' professionals? It may indicate methods of developing systematic ways of giving praise when it is merited – but what about teachers who do not seem to merit praise? The kind of leadership advocated so far highlights a selection of specific approaches that are applicable to a range of what research has revealed to be some of the most common issues relating to teachers' attitudes to their work. However, this does not, of course, include every potential issue nor every possible situation or set of circumstances. What is needed, to supplement the picture built up so far, is a more general set of guidelines for motivational leadership. This chapter provides it.

As I point out in Chapter 2, I do not feel there is much to be gained by prescribing what may be categorized as leadership 'styles'. My preference is for developing an ideological framework for leadership that is likely to motivate – a framework for adopting a general attitude towards leadership that incorporates consideration of guiding principles based upon awareness of key issues and an appropriate ideological stance. The specific framework that I advocate is one based upon what I refer to as a 'teacher-centred' leadership ideology.

What is 'teacher-centred' leadership?

Imagine the following classroom scenario:

The pupils are all engaged on the same task; that of producing coloured patterns of tessellated shapes on squared paper. These are intended to be mounted as a wall display which, it is hoped, will impress parents and other visitors to the school at a forthcoming open day. The teacher has no clear idea of the full potential, or the function, of tessellation as a mathematical topic, but believes the patterns will look very attractive.

The teacher spends most of the time sitting at her desk, engaged on routine tasks, many of which are administrative, and children come out at intervals to show their work or ask questions. The teacher shows little interest in what the children are doing, and breaks off from what she is doing for just long enough to respond to queries about what to do next, or to give permission for children to sharpen pencils, get a second sheet of paper, or go to the toilet. So engrossed is she in her own work that she fails to notice several children who are not 'on task', who are spending long periods daydreaming, misbehaving, or wandering around the room. The children have been given insufficient guidance on how to do the exercise, and, as a result, many of them find the task hard and are making mistakes. Some, on the other hand, clearly have a good grasp of what is required and are creating accurate tessellated patterns which are much more complicated than the teacher would have thought them capable of, and more imaginative than she herself would have managed. When these are shown to her, however, the teacher remains relatively unimpressed. No praise is given in response to children's showing their efforts. Completed patterns are simply placed in a box on the teacher's desk. When she comes to mount the wall display, though, the teacher finds that several patterns are unfinished and many are incorrect, because there are spaces where the shapes actually failed to tessellate. The display is inadequate, unvaried, untidy and generally unimpressive. The teacher sighs, and blames the children.

This scenario could easily be applicable to the primary sector and – if the last sentence of the first paragraph is removed – it could also serve as a depiction of a secondary school mathematics lesson.

To those whose educational ideologies veer towards child-centredness, the deficiencies in this hypothetical teaching situation are easily identifiable. The teacher failed to give adequate direction and guidance to the children before, and throughout, the lesson. Children's individual learning needs, ability levels, and interests were insufficiently accommodated, or even considered. Pupils were treated as a class, rather than as individuals. Their efforts went unrecognized, no interest was shown in what they were doing, and the teacher lacked a general awareness of what was really going on in her classroom.

Most headteachers or principals would consider themselves very unfortunate to have amongst their colleagues a teacher like the one described, who clearly fails to get the best out of the pupils in her care. Yet, on a different level, but in precisely the same way, head-teachers and other school leaders may be equally deficient in managing their teacher colleagues. Indeed, in other chapters I have included illustrations of school management and leadership that is perceived by those who represent the 'managed' to be as deficient as the class management described in the hypothetical case above. Taking this hypothetical scenario bit by bit, let us now examine how it might parallel some forms of staff leadership and management.

The pupils are all engaged on the same task: that of producing coloured patterns of tessellated shapes on squared paper. This illustrates the teacher's neglect of the children's individual learning needs, and the school or department leadership parallel to this would obviously be a neglect of teachers' individual professional development needs, areas of expertise or specific interests. If teachers' individualism is to be accommodated, this may often lead to non-conformity and idiosyncratic ways of working. It may lead to more experimental approaches being tried and to an increase in innovation. Allowing teachers to be individuals involves allowing them the freedom to break the mould and to depart from school or departmental standard practice or policy. But if, at the end of the day, this does not dilute the standard of education that is offered, it should pose no problems. In fact, what may very likely result are enhancements and improvements that may be taken on board more widely. Motivational leadership does not insist on uniformity in relation to ways of working: it celebrates the rich diversity that teachers, as individuals, bring to their work.

These are intended to be mounted as a wall display which, it is hoped, will impress parents and other visitors to the school at a forthcoming open day. The teacher has no clear idea of the full potential, or the function, of tessellation as a mathematical topic, but believes the patterns will look very attractive. This illustrates the teacher's concern for appearances at the expense of a concern for a sound educational rationale for the activities to which she directs children. The obvious parallel in a school or department leadership context is a concern for how things look, rather than their educational benefits. It was for precisely this kind of superficiality that – in the context of my own research – Mrs Hillman, the Leyburn headteacher, was criticized by the Leyburn teacher interviewees. Mark's comments in Chapter 3 indicate the level of his dissatisfaction with this aspect of Mrs Hillman's management of the school. He also said:

> We have a curriculum file which would probably be second to none in the County, because it's got aims and objectives and everything's written down and it's all related to the latest educational documents, but if you go into the classrooms people are performing how they've performed for the last twenty years ... children are still copying off the blackboard ... reading in a fashion which means that children are barking at the words and getting the words right and getting high reading scores, but they're not compre-hending ... and, to me, that's where the leadership falls down.
> *Interviewer: Yes. Does she know this is going on?*
> She doesn't give a shit! Er ... and when Roger Westholme got into ... well, when people were reporting him for poor teaching ... when they were saying that some of his kids hadn't made any progress in maths during the year ... and people, sort of, put pressure on her to have a word with him – unless it was him just being blasé and not admitting to the truth – but he told me that she wasn't interested; she just had a word with him because she had to be *seen* to be having a word with him ... she more or less said, 'Carry on'. She's not *concerned.* (Mark, Leyburn teacher)

Ann also criticized what she considered to be Mrs Hillman's over-concern for the fabric of the school, at the expense of pedagogic issues:

> She'll check the record books, and she'll check that everybody's where they should be, and she'll frown on you if she sees you walking around anywhere when you should be in your room and nowhere else ... but the actual *content* of what you're doing ... I don't think she bothers one jot! ... In fact, I would say my main criticism of her ... is that she's too much wrapped up in the fabric of the school ... the actual bricks and mortar ... and the fact that the toilets are operating. ... I know all these things matter ... and I know it *does* matter that the environment you provide for the children is a good one ... but I think ... er ... *that* seems to matter more than the work. So long as she has curriculum guidelines there, and your schemes of work ... I mean, you could be doing a weekly liar ... if, on paper, everything fulfilled all the criteria ... if all your records and everything fulfilled – so that if anyone from County Hall came in, it would all be there ... I think *that's* what matters ... and I don't *feel* that she's unduly concerned about ... er ... what's going on. (Ann, Leyburn teacher)

And Fiona corroborated Mark's and Ann's perceptions:

> *Interviewer. Now, does Mrs Hillman have an actual educational ideology? Are there*
> *aims and objectives that are adhered to throughout the school?*
> No ... I think it's just all on paper ... but she aims to have a tidy school ...
> her aim is that school does not reflect the outside world ... so there's no
> litter ... no graffiti. ... *That* is what riles her ... untidiness, or wall displays
> that haven't been changed – that's very important to her.
> *Interviewer. Would you say that she's over-bothered about that, to the detriment of*
> *other things?*
> Yes.
> *Interviewer. And do you think that the children's education is neglected, by her, in*
> *favour of that?*
> I think it is, yes.

Just as the good, child-centred teacher would be concerned about
the educational value of the activities that are going on in her/his
classroom, so, too, is good leadership identifiable – in part – by a
concern for the substance of what is going on in her/his school or
department.

The teacher spends most of the time sitting at her desk, engaged on routine
tasks, many of which are administrative, and children come out at intervals
to show their work or ask questions. The teacher shows little interest in what the
children are doing, and breaks off from what she is doing for just long enough
to respond to queries about what to do next, or to give permission for children
to sharpen pencils, get a second sheet of paper, or go to the toilet. This lack of
interest in what the children are doing, which stems from a preoccupation with administrative and other non-teaching work, is
paralleled by leadership that is over-concerned with form-filling,
report writing, and other tasks that distract attention from the real
function and purpose of schools. Some of the Leyburn teachers'
comments above include reference to Mrs Hillman's tendency to be
so preoccupied with administration. Added to these are:

> The things you can rely on her [Mrs Hillman] for – and these are her good
> points – the school has a system ... now, I'm very disorganized and scruffy
> about my person ... but, to run a school efficiently, you've got to have a
> system and you've got to have things labelled and colour-coded. I've given
> her endless notes and photocopies of things, and I've lost my own and,
> when she's not been there, I've gone to her filing cabinet and I can
> guarantee that she'd have it filed away correctly and I could just go and put
> my finger on it. And for all these things she's excellent. But ... she's paid as
> a *leader* ... she's paid as a headteacher ... she's paid as an intellectual ...
> and her clerical duties are only a small aspect of her job. It's what you
> define as 'leadership'. Leadership is ... the main thing is that it can
> influence other people's behaviour and performance, and ... she doesn't
> *really* change anyone's performance because it's purely a paper exercise.
> (Mark, Leyburn teacher)

I like people to be interested in what's going on ... with the kids.

Interviewer. Do you think Mrs Hillman has the children's interests at heart? Is she interested in the education that is going on?

I think she likes to make sure she provides a lot of equipment ... and good teachers ... but, otherwise ... I don't know ... I don't know if she has the academic interests of the kids at heart, to be honest ... I really don't. Because, if she *did* she would ensure that she would be there to help in the classrooms, rather than in the office. (Fiona, Leyburn teacher)

So engrossed is she in her own work that she fails to notice several children who are not 'on task', who are spending long periods daydreaming, misbehaving, or wandering around the room. The children have been given insufficient guidance on how to do the exercise, and, as a result, many of them find the task hard and are making mistakes. This aspect of the teacher's class management is paralleled by school leaders' failure to provide adequate direction and supervision, which may result in some members of staff floundering, struggling, or even slacking. Nias's (1989, p. 107) study revealed teachers to be dissatisfied with *laissez-faire* leadership that offered no clear direction:

> Nearly a quarter of those interviewed indicated that they wanted to be kept up to standard by informed supervision. Their comments ranged from the vividly general ('In a system where you aren't supervised, the bad eggs run riot') to the self-critically specific ('After three years I decided to leave. The head never appeared in the classroom, never kept a check on anything we did. I was getting too good at papering over things, and he didn't notice', or 'By Christmas I needed to be told to put things right, and wasn't strong enough to do it on my own. I'd got into very bad habits and really would have appreciated it if the head had come in and told me so').

Moreover, the case presented in Chapter 2 of the Rockville headteacher's failure to provide supervision of – and to act to remedy – the way in which the deputy head carried out her responsibilities is another example of inadequate direction. Effective leadership, like effective teaching, needs to incorporate mechanisms for directing people in the way in which they ought to be going – without stifling individuals who may wish to go along a different route to get there – and monitoring their progress in doing so.

Some, on the other hand, clearly have a good grasp of what is required and are creating accurate tessellated patterns which are much more complicated than the teacher would have thought them capable of, and more imaginative than she herself would have managed. When these are shown to her, however, the teacher remains relatively unimpressed. This illustration of the teacher's failure to recognize, cater for, and appreciate the exceptional ability of some children is paralleled by school and department leaders' failure to recognize the value of, and to support, 'extended' professionals and exceptionally competent practitioners who manifest particular strengths. My own research evidence of this is presented in Chapter 3. Nias (1989) found similar evidence:

> Many of my interviewees expressed a need for referential support on specifically educational issues. ... Unfortunately, at some point in their careers, the majority of them found themselves in a school in which there was no person or group ... to whom they could turn for self-confirmation in relation to their educational goals. Lacking a reference group in their own schools, they therefore actively sought for one elsewhere. They went on courses. ... As one put it: 'I don't care whether or not the rest of the staff approves of what I'm doing, but I do wish I had someone to discuss my ideas with. I'm so desperate I've signed up for a course at the Polytechnic'. (p. 48)

> Although many of these teachers initially tried to find, within their schools, colleagues who would support them in their view of themselves as people who valued ideas and intellectual debate, they felt that they seldom met with a sympathetic response. The cumulative effect of repeated rebuffs (as they saw the failure of their efforts to stimulate staffroom discussion to be) was to force them back into contact with established reference groups outside their schools and eventually to alienate them from teaching. ... Overall, in the early interviews about two-thirds talked of wanting to leave the classroom eventually, because, as one woman put it, 'My mind feels starved'. (p. 49)

In the same way that effective teachers take every opportunity to 'stretch' and challenge students of exceptional ability – and, indeed, facilitate every child's achieving his/her full potential – so, too, must effective school leadership involve enabling, rather than constraining and frustrating, teachers.

No praise is given in response to children's showing their efforts. Completed patterns are simply placed in a box on the teacher's desk. The parallel with school leadership here is obvious. Just as teachers praise children for their achievements because they believe it will encourage and spur them on to sustained – and increased – effort, so, too, does motivational school leadership incorporate recognition of teachers' work and much positive feedback on their efforts and achievements.

When she comes to mount the wall display, though, the teacher finds that several patterns are unfinished and many are incorrect, because there are spaces where the shapes actually failed to tessellate. The display is inadequate, unvaried, untidy and generally unimpressive. The teacher sighs, and blames the children. My purpose in including these last sentences in the allegorical classroom scenario is to point out the potential impact of ineffective school leadership, leadership that fails to get the best out of teachers. The results are very likely to be as unimpressive as the wall display that the teacher hoped to produce, but to which she did not devote enough care, attention and effort. In relation to school leadership – unless you are particularly lucky in having an excellent, self-motivated and highly talented staff who are prepared, for a time, to carry on unstintingly in the face of difficulties and constraints – you reap what you sow.

If headteachers and other school leaders are to get the best out of teachers it is clear that much can be learned from examination of teacher–pupil relations. Most school leaders are capable of recognizing and appreciating effective teaching: teaching that puts children's interests paramount and incorporates consideration of their different developmental needs. Most understand and accept the child-centred ideological principles upon which such teaching is based, realizing that they provide the key to getting the best out of children. Yet many of these same leaders fail to make the obvious connection that a system of effectively 'leading' children is equally applicable to the leadership of adults. In this sense, they operate according to dual standards, and they often fail to see the inconsistency and irrationality of this, about which, in relation to the issue of providing feedback to teachers, Nias (1989, pp. 147-8) comments: 'It seems strange that institutions built upon the rhetoric (and very often the reality) of caring for children should be so poor at giving recognition to adults'. Indeed, the relevance for staff management of class management techniques was highlighted by several of my interviewees, who commented on the similarity of their own motivational needs to those of children. As Kay, a Sefton Road teacher, pointed out: 'Oh, I think teachers are just the same – they need just as much encouragement as children'.

Applying the predominantly child-centred primary school class management approach – which has been prevalent in the UK from the 1960s – to the context of staff management creates a parallel approach which I refer to as 'teacher-centred'.

A framework for a 'teacher-centred' approach to school management and leadership

To become 'teacher-centred' in their approach to staff management by applying a 'child-centred' parallel, school leaders need to consider themselves as, effectively, class teachers on a larger scale. They need to consider their schools or departments as their classrooms writ large, and their teacher colleagues as their classes of pupils or students, in a more mature state. This involves adopting a 'teacher-centred' leadership philosophy and incorporating into their management an organizational structure that reflects this.

Adopting a 'teacher-centred' philosophy

Many of the headteachers identified and described in my study evidently either were unaware of the extent to which their leadership was capable of influencing teachers' attitudes, or had neither the time nor the inclination to provide positive leadership. It is conceivable that some may either believe or feel that it should be the case that teachers, since they are responsible adults, should be self-motivated. A lot of teachers are, indeed, self-motivated, but there is no reason to avoid augmenting their motivation or boosting their morale by a few well-chosen words.

Analysis of my research findings reveals five key features of motivational leadership: *individualism, recognition, awareness, interest* and *direction*; precisely the features of class management which were lacking in the hypothetical classroom scenario presented above. As I have illustrated in earlier chapters, despite their greater maturity than that of children, teachers respond well to the kind of leadership which incorporates many of the features of effective class teaching and management. A 'teacher-centred' philosophy to primary school staff management acknowledges the importance of these five foci.

Individualism

As I have already emphasized – and illustrated – teachers are not all the same. They are, of course, different in temperament and aptitude, age, experience and subject interests, and in relation to ability, commitment and professionality. Each teacher will have individual needs which reflect his/her educational ideologies and values. Most teachers will lie somewhere between the two extremes of 'restricted' and 'extended' professionality, and a school staff and, in many cases, a school department will typically include a mixture of teachers, reflecting a wide range of different professionality orientations. The challenge for school leaders is to value this individuality by trying to accommodate these varied needs as far as it is possible, without compromising the needs of the school as a whole, just as a conscientious teacher will offer a differentiated curriculum. 'Extended' professionals may need to be involved in decision-making, for example, or would appreciate being consulted about policy development. 'Restricted' professionals may be very effective classroom practitioners who need to feel valued in their role. To motivate staff on an individual level, school leaders need to see teachers as individuals, rather than as a corporate whole. The comments of a primary school headteacher who has evidently taken on board the need for individualism highlight the key principles of this feature of 'teacher-centred' leadership:

I just feel I am able to see people and put their behaviour in the context and see their motives for the way they behave. You are able to distance yourself from it and know it is not you. It is human nature and due to a variety of reasons ... I think my own repertoire of skills and my own approach to understanding what motivates the staff has developed. You learn that as you go along. The same thing is not going to appeal to everybody. I try and make judgements about how different people work and I try and work on those particular accents of their own personality. So I work very differently with different people and my own approach changes depending on who it is I am talking to and who I am working with. . . . It is also about getting to know people and that takes time. I spend a lot of time talking to people and getting to know how teacher A and teacher B works, what their particular hang-ups and obsessions are, and what their particular needs are, and I try to meet those in a way that is possible ... I think fundamentally I believe in people as well as myself. (Pascal and Ribbins, 1998, p. 203)

It is not only teachers' professionality that is reflected in their individual needs. Steers *et al.* (1996, p. 3) highlight the complex and multifaceted derivation of the individualism that members bring to an organization:

Individual organizational membership is segmented in nature in the sense that people belong to other groups (e.g. families) or organizations (e.g. churches), in addition to their work organizations. Furthermore, people have powerful experiences over the course of their lives (e.g. college education, raising children). The pattern and intensity of people's motives may change as they assimilate their continuing experiences. These changing needs and motives may result in behaviors, such as an expressed desire for greater independence and autonomy, that require some kind of response from the organization, a response that cannot always be handled by its existing structural features. *Leadership, then, is proposed as a process to enable the organization to accommodate these kinds of individual predispositions and tendencies* [my emphasis].

Applying a 'teacher-centred' approach to staff leadership and management involves incorporating consideration of competing pressures in teachers' lives and demands on their time and attention. The 'teacher-centred' leader recognizes the advantages and rewards of enabling rather than constraining teachers by management that responds to their needs in much the same way as that of, and with much the same attitude as that underpinning, a child-centred teacher's responses to her/his pupils' or students' needs. The 'teacher-centred' leader adopts a 'child-centred' frame of reference to her/his dealings with staff, asking her/himself, at each appropriate opportunity, 'How would I handle this person if s/he were a child in my class?'

An example from my own research of staff management that failed to incorporate a concern for individualism is that of Phil, the Sefton

Road headteacher. Certainly, Phil was, by far, the most motivational of the three headteachers in whose schools I observed, and elsewhere in this book I have illustrated some of the more effective features of his leadership. Yet Phil's leadership was also marked by an intolerance of those who failed to conform to his notion of a good practitioner. To varying degrees, as he told me in conversation, he was happy with most of the staff, and most of them had been appointed by him. He chose teachers with care, and with a view to transforming the school from what he had, at the time of his appointment to the headship eight years ago, considered to be an outmoded, lacklustre institution, staffed, in the main, by 'old guard' 'restricted' professionals, into a vibrant, exciting, 'on-the-ball' type of school. Those who had witnessed his progress generally agreed that Phil had 'turned the school around', though rather more through a process of erosion than of explosion, but with sufficient forcefulness to ease out, one way or another, most of the teachers who did not share his clear vision.

One teacher who did not share Phil's vision and who, as a result, found herself out of favour with him, was Louise. Louise did not have permanent status. She taught full-time and had responsibility for a Year 5 class (9–10-year-olds) but, when I interviewed her, she was employed on a one-year temporary contract, having spent a large proportion of the previous year as a supply teacher at Sefton Road. She was interviewed in the summer of 1990, shortly before her temporary contract was due to expire. She was going to leave Sefton Road at the end of the school year, and had been appointed to a school in the private sector.

I would categorize Louise as a 'restricted' professional. Her teaching was intuitively-based and generally reflected a low level of classroom competence and organizational efficiency. Her lessons were not always well-planned, nor well thought-out, and her teaching in its entirety lacked coherence in its structure. She did not seem to be committed to any specific educational ideologies or principles. She took little interest in school policy and organization.

Louise seemed to enjoy teaching and, in her own way, was quite conscientious. She was pleasant, good-natured and cooperative. She established a good rapport with her pupils and managed their behaviour reasonably successfully, but her commitment to and engagement in her work was probably lower than that of my other interviewees. The effort that she expended on the job was by no means exceptionally low: indeed, she seemed to consider herself quite hard-working, and, had she been employed at another school, rather than at Sefton Road, she might not necessarily have been noticeably different from her colleagues in relation to commitment, conscientiousness and competence. At Rockville, for example, she would not have stood out from the crowd. At Sefton Road, though, with its hard-working, competitive climate (described briefly in Chapter 5), Louise was like a fish out of water.

Louise was well-liked on a personal level by many of her colleagues, even though on a professional level it was generally recognized that, within the school's professional culture, she was, in effect, a deviant. She was included in whatever staffroom camaraderie there was time for, within the pervasive busyness and work-related focus of activity, and she sometimes socialized with colleagues after school. She valued her personal life higher than she did her working life and established clear parameters of what she was prepared to accept as the demands of the job. She was not happy at work. She was most dissatisfied with the management of Sefton Road and with the headteacher's leadership. It failed to motivate her and, throughout the time she spent there, until she was appointed to a new post, her morale was low.

Louise blamed her negative job-related attitudes on Phil. She found the school's professional climate, which she attributed to Phil's leadership style, very uncomfortable. It was too demanding and stressful for her and, more particularly, it required of teachers a level of commitment, conscientiousness and industriousness that she considered excessive. Working at Sefton Road, in Louise's view, involved a level of effort that exceeded the parameters of acceptability that she had drawn up for herself. She provided an example of a particular incident that highlighted the very different expectations held by Phil and herself of the demands of teaching at Sefton Road:

> ... they were having this Asian week ... so, everything had to be done for this, and he [Phil] was very worked up about it ... he wanted everything to be absolutely wonderful. But, you see, when I came into that classroom it was bare ... totally bare ... so I had to start from scratch. ... I got one full board covered, but then he came in and he said, 'Oh, you'll have to come in at the weekend and you'll have to fill all the boards – all the lot – because it's Asian week next week and it's *got* to be done'. So he gave me a key and then he took me round to Mary's classroom, and he said, 'Now, do look around and get ideas from other classes'. And he said, 'I know you're on your own and, as you know, Mary is. Maybe you don't feel as she does, with you only being here for a year, but, you see, she's doing all these cushions for the children ... you know ... sort of ... doing them at night'. ... Well, I was just ... gobsmacked ... utterly – I was dumbstruck. I just thought, 'Who the heck do you think you are?' ... I wish I could've come back at him and said, 'I'm sorry; I've got a personal life ... '. And I know Mary's on her own, but she's making school her whole *life*. ... But ... I mean ... he'd no right to say that to me. It was assuming ... really ... putting me down ... and I was quite horrified by it.

It was clear that Louise neither shared nor supported Phil's vision of how he wanted the school to develop. She found the climate of hard work and competitiveness oppressive and incomprehensible. It was entirely alien to her:

> ... if I'd been at Sefton Road when I was actually assessed for my probationary year I just couldn't have coped. I believe Phil has you doing lesson plans *all the time* when you're a probationer – whereas I only did them when the adviser was coming in.
>
> ... I feel that he uses his staff to the utmost – I don't know why they all work so hard ... and it's all for the glorification of *him* ... and I don't like that either. But everybody runs around for him like chickens with their heads cut off – they're not like human beings; they're like automatons ... and everybody's like that because of ... the pressure ... which I've never found in any other school ... and I've worked in enough!
>
> *Interviewer: So, you'd say there was a distinct climate?*
>
> Oh, yes!
>
> *Interviewer: How would you describe it?*
>
> Well ... I find it stressful ... a stressful climate ... I mean ... there are only so many hours in a day ... and I feel that, with Phil, he wants 110 per cent off everybody ... and I think that's asking too much. ... Actually, d'you know what I think it is? ... I think it's a bit of 'keeping up with the Jones's'. Everybody wants to do better than everybody else ... it's almost ... like on a street, or whatever. I've come across these people who have to 'keep up with the Jones's' ... they're a certain type of person that does it – I'm not one of them, of course – and sometimes I think there's a lot of this rivalry ... wanting to do better than the others have done.

Moreover, Louise was extremely cynical of Phil's motives. In most respects, her views of Phil and of working at Sefton Road contrasted strikingly with those of most of her colleagues, including Sarah and Kay, whose comments are presented in other chapters. In their interviews, Sarah and Kay had remarked on how pedagogically sound they considered Phil to be, and of his great concern for the children's welfare and education. Louise's perspective was quite distinct from theirs. She spoke of Phil:

> Personally, I think he's just interested in creating a good show ... but that's personal and I might be wrong ... but that's the impression I've been given ... that the most important thing to Phil is to put on a good show.
>
> *Interviewer: Do you think he has the children's interests at heart?*
>
> No ... no. I know he's very *good* with them ... er ... no ... I don't think he's interested in their well-being – he definitely wants to create a good show, to impress people coming in – it's definitely, to me, a show school ... to impress other people.

She then described an incident that, she felt, illustrated her point:

> We were all having to put up some displays with an ecology theme, and I got this idea from Jill which Jill thought was okay ... but ... again, I made the

mistake of having *all* the children doing art work. They were doing three things. First of all they were starting off with a pencil drawing, doing an abstract design ... then they had to copy it in paint, and then, again, in chalk. It was such hard work, but, again, if I'd known the school then, as I do now, I would've simply taken my six best artists and let *them* do work for the display. So I eventually managed to pick out the best and pinned them up on the wall outside – and they were there for two days, pinned up. Then I stapled them one night, and the following morning he [Phil] came in ... and he was genuinely embarrassed ... and he called me out of the classroom and he said, 'I'm sorry, but it's not good enough, so it's got to come down'. And he said, 'But, don't worry, Jill's going to put some stuff there'. Well, I was just absolutely demoralized – *totally* demoralized!
Interviewer. Why was it not good enough, did he say?
Well, looking at other work ... he just said, 'For Year 5, it's not good enough. It's not professional enough'. And I realized that when I saw other people's work, but I realized what they'd done ... they'd just taken the best. It has to be 'top show', and you've to pick out your best children and get *them* to do something. And, to me, I, personally, don't like that ... because I don't like top show. But, alright, the work produced was *super* ... but, again, it's *knowing* what to do. I was just lost.

Louise was desperately unhappy at Sefton Road, and was anxious to leave as soon as she possibly could. On one occasion, after Phil's manner with her had upset her, she had complained to the LEA's Director of Education and asked for a transfer to another school. She told me that her request had been very sympathetically received, but the Director had flattered her, told her that she was strong enough to cope, and, very kindly, persuaded her to remain at Sefton Road.

She spoke of her relief that she had secured another post, obviating the need for her to remain at Sefton Road: 'I couldn't *bear* to go back there. I couldn't bear it'. When she summed up her attitude to her job at Sefton Road, it was, once again, on Phil that Louise focused, attributing her low level of job engagement to him: 'You see, I cannot give my all to somebody that I don't like and respect. That says it all, really'.

The point is that Phil failed to get the best out of Louise because he failed to accommodate her individuality. His leadership certainly did incorporate a degree of what I refer to as individualism, but only in respect of those teachers whom he liked and of whom he approved because, essentially, they shared and supported his vision. These – the majority of the staff, in fact – were allowed and encouraged to be inventive and adventurous. Often they were indulged. But Louise was not. Phil did not disguise his disapproval of what he considered to be her unconscientious attitude and her unimpressive practice. He did not apply 'teacher-centred' leadership to her. He did not respond to her as he would have if she had been a child in his class. If he had done, he would have been much more inclined to encourage her by manifesting approval of and appreciation for any of her behaviour that approximated – however slightly – to the kind of behaviour that he wanted her to exhibit. He would have appreciated the need to compromise, and would have tried to win her over gradually. Instead, he conveyed criticism and disapproval, and he alienated her entirely. His effectiveness as a leader was therefore diluted because – although he motivated many – he failed to reach all of the Sefton Road staff.

Recognition
It is clear that teachers, like children, need recognition of their efforts. The positive effects of a leadership approach that incorporated recognition of teachers' work are demonstrated, in the context of my research (see Chapter 5), by the case of Sefton Road Primary School. Leyburn County Primary School's case, in contrast, highlights the detrimental effects on teachers' attitudes towards working at the school of leadership that failed to incorporate recognition.

'Teacher-centred' management and leadership recognizes teachers' efforts through positive feedback and, in particular, through praise. Recognition is a key motivator because of the important part that it plays in the job fulfilment process, as illustrated in my model presented in Chapter 5. Recognition reinforces the individual's image of her/his 'self-at-work' and, in particular, of the effectiveness with which work-related tasks are carried out.

To achieve maximum effectiveness as a leadership tool, recognition must incorporate individualism. Applying consideration of the child-centred class management parallel highlights the importance of ensuring that personalized, individual recognition of efforts is fair and equitable. This does not mean that it should be applied in a systematic, sequential way to everyone in turn. This would render it practically useless by implicitly removing the meritocratic principles that underpin it. What it does mean, though, is that, just as a child-centred teacher would endeavour to try to find something praiseworthy about all of her/his pupils' work and to guard against directing too frequent and repeated praise at some children whilst leaving others feeling comparatively deprived of praise, so, too, should a 'teacher-centred' headteacher exercise similar care and solicitude for teachers' feelings in recognizing their efforts. In this respect, though, an advantage that is afforded headteachers in their management of staff over teachers' management of classes, is that much of the personalized, individual attention and, in particular, recognition that s/he may want to direct at some teachers may, through careful management, be obscured from others. Teachers are less likely to disclose to colleagues than children are to their classmates that they have been singled out for special recognition or praise.

Awareness

In order to recognize teachers' efforts, though, school and departmental heads need to be aware of what is going on in their schools and departments. This should not be a vague, general awareness. It involves having an overview of what is happening in every classroom (in the case of primary schools) or in every year group across the different subjects (in the case of secondary schools). The 'aware' primary school head or principal will know, for example, what topic each class is doing, and what work is being done in different subjects. The 'aware' secondary school head will know which specific physical education activities are offered to which year groups, which Shakespeare play is being studied by which year groups, and what kind of activities go on in the Special Educational Needs unit. This awareness needs to be conveyed to teachers if it is to be an effective motivator. Taking in weekly planning books and initialling them is not enough: the headteacher or head of department needs to comment upon teachers' written plans, either orally or in written form, and, ideally, also needs to be seen to be aware of what is going on when s/he moves around the school doing routine tasks. Explicit references need to be included in conversations, to demonstrate this 'awareness'. As I have illustrated in earlier chapters, headteachers who were 'unaware' of what was going on were heavily criticized by the teachers involved in my study, and much dissatisfaction and demotivation was attributed to them. Helen, for example, criticized her headteacher at Woodleigh Lane for his failure to know the names of the children in the school and to be able to comment on their progress:

> He doesn't collect in any planning books, he doesn't know what people are teaching! He hasn't a clue! . . . I mean, he doesn't know the children . . . he doesn't know the children by name. He's written a comment on their reports that've gone home yesterday . . . and he's put exactly the same comment on every child's report, because he doesn't know them. He doesn't know who they are.

In contrast, Nias *et al.* (1989, p. 108) describe the kind of awareness that characterized leadership of those schools in their study that manifested collaborative cultures:

> Much of this awareness was made possible because the heads were constantly around the school and visited everyone or were around when staff gathered together. . . . These visits were brief, but supportive, with the head often smiling and encouraging the discussion of classroom or personal matters. . . . The implicit message in much of this is the head's accessibility. The heads were not only approachable but available. They did not simply wait to hear about things; by touring the school, being in the staffroom and visiting teachers in their classrooms or class areas they actively sought out news and information. The heads were expert at noticing all sorts of seemingly small matters.

Awareness involves knowing about significant events, situations and circumstances, both in school and out of school, that may affect teachers' and pupils' lives. The 'aware' primary school head, deputy head, or secondary school departmental head knows the names of teachers' partners and children, for example, and, in the case of children, knows their approximate age, whether they are about to go to university, get married, or start school or work. S/he knows, too, about arguments, disagreements or sources of conflict between staff, and s/he puts this knowledge to good effect by incorporating into her/his management consideration of the effects that such things may have upon teachers. The 'aware' secondary school head makes sure that s/he is kept up to date about such information by having it passed on by senior teachers. The 'teacher-centred' leader combines individualism with awareness in order to perceive, and treat, teachers as people, rather than as units of a whole staff.

Interest

An interest in individual teachers' work, as it translates into students' and pupils' learning, goes hand-in-hand with awareness and is equally important for school leaders to demonstrate. My research shows teachers to be very sensitive to headteachers' and other senior teachers' apparent lack of interest in the children's education. This often occurred when heads were keen administrators and ran well-organized schools, as was the case with Mrs Hillman at Leyburn. It also occurred when heads were perceived as generally inadequate for the role of headship, as was the case with Helen's headteacher at Woodleigh Lane.

Headteachers' and other school leaders' interest in teachers' work is a key influence on teachers' job fulfilment since it may contribute towards strengthening their perceptions of their work as valuable and worthwhile. The extent of its influence is affected by other factors, such as the headteacher's credibility and status as leading professional (Coulson, 1988, p. 258), which I examine in the next chapter, and teachers' own self-esteem. Selective interest on the part of respected headteachers towards specific components of teachers' work may – particularly in the case of inexperienced teachers, who may lack self-confidence – impede their deriving job fulfilment from other elements of the work. The headteacher who, for example, manifests a much keener interest in the academic progress of a group of very able children than in the less impressive targets reached by a child with special needs, is conveying implicit values-laden messages to teachers.

Direction

Child-centred education has been criticized by its detractors on the grounds that, in its most extreme progressive form, it is characterized by chaotic organization and unstructured classroom activities that produce superficial or insufficient learning. Certainly, if it lacks adequate teacher direction, it can degenerate into chaos. But it need not be so. Child-centred education is, paradoxically, most successful when it is rigidly managed and skilfully coordinated and directed by the teacher.

By the same token, 'teacher-centred' school leadership is most effective when it incorporates clear direction towards the realization of a shared vision of what the school should become. The leader's role in providing direction is emphasized by Steers *et al.* (1996, p. 3):

> ... the organization, as a formal and abstract blueprint (of sorts), is necessarily imperfect because actual human behavior is infinitely more complex and variable than any 'plan' could accommodate. An organizational design cannot possibly account for every member's activity at all times. Consequently, in addition to various structural features, organizations must possess a mechanism that can ensure human behavior is coordinated and directed toward task accomplishment. *That mechanism is presumed to be leadership* [my emphasis].

My research revealed much dissatisfaction on the part of teachers with heads who, by failing to provide adequate direction, left staff with a sense of lack of purpose. Where headteachers' failure to provide direction was interpreted as apathy and laziness, or as an abrogation of responsibilities for which they were being paid, teachers were particularly resentful. Helen, for example, spoke of her head at Woodleigh Lane:

> I mean ... part of it is ... I mean, this is the very, very lowest ... level ... but I do resent the fact that he draws that salary. ... And, I mean, he draws £25,000 a year ... for doing sod-all ... and I resent that. That offends my sense of justice ... you know, when there are teachers who work a lot harder and get a lot less, and all that kind of issue.

Summarizing 'teacher-centred' leadership

Adopting a 'teacher-centred' approach to school leadership involves applying a wider perspective to the job than has traditionally been applied. It requires acceptance that, in the work context, there are two groups of people – rather than just one – for whose development and well-being you share responsibility: two groups whose interests you try to promote and whose needs you try to meet. 'Teacher-centred' school leadership is not just about working with teaching – and other – colleagues to work for the good of the children in your care. It is also about adding to what you accept as your responsibilities a second tier of care and solicitude: one that is directed at these colleagues. It is about working for the good of teachers.

Make no mistake – 'teacher-centred' leadership is not weak leadership. On the contrary, it provides leaders with the mechanisms for developing their competence and, through this, strengthening their own positions and credibility. 'Teacher-centred' leadership is perfectly compatible with the demands currently being made of school leaders in the UK – with the 'push' towards strong leadership being emphasized in the 1998 Green Paper (DfEE, 1998):

> Good heads are crucial to the success of schools. We need to develop strong leaders. (p. 21)

> All the evidence shows that heads are the key to a school's success. All schools need a leader who creates a sense of purpose and direction, sets high expectations of staff and pupils, focuses on improving teaching and learning, monitors performance and motivates the staff to give of their best. (p. 22)

It is through 'teacher-centred' leadership that staff who might otherwise work against the leadership begin to work with it and, in doing so, increase leaders' strength and capacity. 'Teacher-centred' leaders are able to achieve much more than other school leaders because they take staff with them, rather than leave them behind. Consider, again, the class teacher–pupil parallel. Which of the following two different teaching and class management approaches would impress you by suggesting strength of leadership of pupils or students?

- The teacher – despite her/his authoritarian stance and strict attitude – is unable to control all of the children, with the result that some are not 'on task', some cannot, or will not, do what is required of them, and one or two have been sent out of the room because the teacher has given up on them.
- The teacher is working to provide an environment in which every pupil may achieve some measure of success and achievement in some area. There are a few children in the class who are slow learners, who have special educational needs or who have behaviour problems, but the teacher is making good headway in alleviating these difficulties by trying to provide each child with work that interests him/her and that is at an appropriate level. Through endeavouring to meet as many individual needs as possible, the teacher maintains generally effective class control and has to deal with less disruption than does the

first teacher. Of course, problems do erupt from time to time, but the teacher deals with them by focusing on the needs of the individuals who created them. No child has had to be sent out of the room for misbehaviour and there is an atmosphere of busyness and enjoyment, with many more children 'on task' than in the first teacher's classroom.

Now, reapply to these scenarios a school leadership parallel, and decide whether real leadership strength is, in the long run, achieved by authoritarianism and rigidity, or by compromise, consideration and concern for others.

CHAPTER 7

Motivating through credibility: The leading professional

Introduction

There is no blueprint for motivating staff. This is because there are so many variables in the process. One of the key variables – which I have already discussed – is the individuality of those whom one wishes to motivate. What I have offered in this book, therefore, is a framework, rather than a blueprint, for motivational leadership. So far, I have provided both specific and general guidelines for ways of managing and leading teaching staff in order to get the best out of them. I have focused on interpersonal aspects of leadership and illustrated effective ways of relating to staff as individuals and as a group. The approaches to leadership that I suggest – and which reflect what I call a 'teacher-centred' ideology – are predominantly concerned with the behaviour and attitudes of school leaders to their teacher colleagues.

Since it is based on what research has revealed teachers want from their leaders, I have no doubt at all that those who model their leadership on this framework will increase their effectiveness at motivating others. What I have not yet dealt with, though, is another key variable in the process of getting the best out of staff – the individuality of the leader.

We have looked at ways in which school leaders ought to behave, and what sorts of attitudes they ought to adopt, but not at their personal and professional characteristics and qualities. It is, of course, very difficult to separate characteristics and personality traits from behaviour because it is through behaviour that they are manifested. Nevertheless, in this chapter I attempt a shift of emphasis from consideration of what leaders *do* towards what they are like. A key factor contributing to the success of school leadership behaviour is one specific aspect of leaders' individuality – their credibility with teachers. The national standards for headteachers in the UK (TTA, 1998, p. 7) include reference to this:

> Headteachers should have the professional competence and expertise to:
> xii. command credibility through the discharge of their functions and to influence others ...

This chapter examines what gives school leaders credibility.

Leader credibility: Personal and professional image

Even following the prescriptive guidelines that I present in this book, the degree of success with which you are able to motivate staff will be greatly influenced by how they perceive you – primarily as a school leader, but also as a person. In particular, leadership effectiveness is affected by four interrelated factors. The first – *credibility as a person* – relates to leaders' personal qualities. The other three relate more to professional characteristics: *credibility as a teacher, credibility as an intellectual,* and *credibility as a leading professional.*

Credibility as a person

It is reasonable to assume that – all other things being equal – the more your teacher colleagues like you as a person, the more they will approve of your leadership and the more effective a leader you will be. It was certainly the case amongst my teacher interviewees that their dislike of specific personality traits in their headteachers reduced the respect that they had for them, which, in turn, impoverished the leader–staff relationship.

Habitual rudeness and short-temperedness on the part of headteachers were criticized by those of my interviewees who had experienced it – although these characteristics did not appear to be prevalent, and none of the headteachers in whose schools I carried out observation were reported by teachers, or observed by me, to exhibit them. Some teachers identified these characteristics in relation to former headteachers:

> But, she was a very stringent person – not very gracious ... again, somebody who couldn't say 'Please' and 'Thank you' ... and she could be a real ... tyrant – *very* unpleasant. She liked *me*, because I used to joke with her ... and I think she used to pick on weaker members of staff and make their lives very unpleasant – until they left. But she didn't pick on *me* – she had the odd 'go' at me ... but nothing much ... because I think she thought that I would perhaps stand up for myself. (Ann, Leyburn teacher)

> Mr Black ... was awful to us – *awful!* He was very bitter ... and we couldn't do anything right. ... You couldn't talk to him about anything ... I mean, he was very rude to people ... he was *awful.* (Joanne, Rockville teacher)

Without doubt, the most despised characteristic identified was dishonesty. Where teachers mistrusted their headteacher – questioned his/her integrity, doubted his/her motives, or suspected him/her of deviousness or duplicity – they seemed to lose faith in his/her leadership. Only one of the Leyburn interviewees referred to the questionability of Mrs Hillman's honesty. Ann spoke of the issue of the Government-imposed directed time of 1265 hours per year for teachers. This had been introduced in the UK in 1987, but it seemed to have been ignored by the majority of headteachers, who, aware that most of their teacher colleagues – of their own free will – already worked considerably longer hours on average than those stipulated by the Government, perceived it as a threat to teacher morale. Mrs Hillman, however, was one of what were – from all accounts – the very few headteachers who insisted on applying the directed hours 'by the book', with the effect of lengthening the *official* working day for teachers. Ann's complaint was that she felt the Leyburn staff had been deceived by Mrs Hillman into accepting that there was no leeway for headteachers to apply discretion over this issue:

> I said my piece about the directed time.
> *Interviewer. Has that affected morale at all – the directed time?*
> Oh, yes! Yes, *very* much! *I* resented it every day! And yet ... and yet, there was many a time when you *would* have stayed until *after* four o'clock ... but the very fact ...
> *Interviewer. Do you find yourself leaving at four now?*
> Well, I *did* – when I was full-time ... *always* ... always went at four! And that's part of my stubbornness – I'm very stubborn. But, you see, I was there at twenty past eight every day – now, that wasn't taken into account ... er ... what about the rounders matches you do ... and the swimming gala ... and, whatever? And the fact that you took them [the pupils] on holiday for a whole week, and ... you know ... it's give and take, isn't it? ... And I think she was very foolish ... and that staff meeting where we discussed it just proved her to be a liar! She was lying through her teeth about things ... about how it had always been flexible, and how she'd had to submit things to the Education Office ... well, it just wasn't true!

Of all the headteachers of whom my interviewees spoke, Geoff Collins was the most frequently and consistently identified as dishonest. Several Rockville teachers made reference to, or provided illustrative accounts of, what they perceived to be his deceitfulness:

> When I first went to Rockville I respected him [Geoff] as a person. I always thought that, whatever he did – even if I disagreed with it – his motives were right ... that he did it from kindness, or a goodness inside him ... but, just recently – and Amanda has said these things to me before and I've 'pooh-poohed' them – about him being dishonest, about him changing things, about him talking to other people about private things that you've said ... but, this last term, I have found the same thing. ... He's downright lied to

me on several occasions, and he's lied about things that I've known about, on several occasions ... and, to me, that's not on. (Pat, Rockville teacher)

I've seen another side of him [Geoff] lately, which I was a bit surprised about, really. You know this business about the Section 11 business[1] – you've heard about that? ... he thought he could just, sort of ... put all the part-timers into that role. He said to us, 'Just think about it. It's just an idea. You know, have a think, consult your unions', which we did. ... In the interim he'd told us that we couldn't be moved out of the town if we were Section 11. ... Well, first of all, Pat brought me a contract which said *specifically* that we *could* be moved anywhere in the County ... specifically written in black and white! ... I think, over the last two years, he's become, probably, more sneaky. (Brenda, Rockville teacher)

He is devious because he passes the buck. ... Like Alison's pointed out to me, he *must* have been devious because he made it look like *her* – we've complained about *her* coming to us and saying such and such, and he'd say, 'Oh, I didn't know about that ... ' when he *has* known about it because he's told her to say it! ... now, it's devious and it's dishonest. ... I think Alison's more professional than either Margaret or Geoff. ... And once I'd realized she was sound, as a person ... from then on I got on really well with her, and if she was critical I could take it from her – like, if she didn't agree with something I'd put in my record book ... or how I'd gone about something ... I could take it then. (Elaine, Rockville teacher)

Elaine's comment above illustrates the positive attitudes on the part of teachers in relation to their leaders that are much more likely to emanate from trust and confidence in their integrity than from mistrust. Any relationship will struggle to flourish amidst dishonesty and deception, and the teacher–school leader relationship is no exception. Geoff's dishonesty manifested itself on several occasions in the course of my observation at Rockville. Sometimes it was very apparent in his attempts – invariably futile – to fob teachers off with excuses, in order to cover up his own mistakes. Under these circumstances it was the lack of openness that the Rockville staff resented. Geoff never – to the best of my knowledge – admitted to having made an error of judgement, nor an unwise decision; he seemed to prefer to try to talk his way out of any disadvantageous situation that resulted. Yet, as many of the Rockville teachers commented, he would have been far better coming clean and saying something like, 'I'm afraid I've done something rather stupid and, as a result, we now find ourselves in the situation ... '. This would almost certainly have resulted in most teachers rallying round to help. Instead, he perpetuated an atmosphere of mistrust, cynicism and disdain.

As a leader, you stand a much better chance of getting teachers on your side – working with rather than against you – if you are, at all times, open and honest with them, than if you shut them out and are

economical with the truth. If you are not by nature open and candid
– if you habitually cover up your emotions and hide your feelings –
you may need to work at this: at least, in relation to your 'self-at-work'.
Most importantly, you need to accept that admitting openly to having
made mistakes is not an indication of your weakness – quite the
contrary. Human nature being as it is, you will invariably strengthen
your own position by enhancing your personal credibility and securing considerably more respect – and help – than if you try to sweep
your mistakes under the carpet.

A particularly interesting finding to emerge from my research was
that, although school leaders' personal characteristics and personality
traits that were disliked by teachers diminished leader credibility,
likeable qualities did not increase the credibility of leaders who were
considered to be deficient in their role. Teachers often distinguished
between certain aspects of personality and of leadership, separating
the 'person' from the headteacher:

> It isn't a job for him [Geoff], really . . . he's not a manager – as a *person*, he's
> very nice – but, as a manager, he's the worst head I've worked for, by a long
> way – a *long* way. (Jean, Rockville teacher)

> As a *person*, I really like him [Geoff], but I don't think, as a head, he's good
> at his job. (Elaine, Rockville teacher)

> Jack McNulty, the head at St Paul's, where I used to be . . . he's grand. . . . I
> mean, he's a nice bloke . . . er . . . I wouldn't say he's super efficient, though
> – but he's very amenable. (Jane, Rockville teacher)

The impression which I gained of the Rockville headteacher's
personality, for example, was that he was both likeable and generally
well-liked. He was, as one of my interviewees described him, 'a nice
bloke'. Yet these qualities were not incorporated into overall assessments of Geoff's leadership, which, as earlier chapters illustrate, were
generally very negative. Rather, in an ambiguous way, they were
identified on the one hand as compensatory or even redeeming
qualities, which served to preclude assessments of Geoff being
entirely negative, and on the other hand as factors which contributed
to what was considered to be Geoff's inadequate leadership. In other
words, many of those aspects of Geoff's character which made him
likeable were, for the most part, given very poor rating as leadership
qualities. More significantly, as the examples of Geoff's leadership
provided in earlier chapters illustrate, headteachers who are liked on
a personal level are just as capable of engendering negative job-
related attitudes amongst their colleagues as those who are not. A
'nice' personality in a headteacher offers no safeguard against staff

dissatisfaction, demotivation and low morale emanating from his/her leadership – nor does it secure his/her credibility as a leader.

Credibility as a teacher

One of the headteachers with whom I worked during my primary school teaching career was clearly a highly intelligent, well-educated man, who was able to complete the *Guardian* crossword within an hour (usually in school time), was very knowledgeable about classical music, and whose powers of reasoning were outstanding. The school that he led was located in an inner city, in an area of extreme poverty and social disadvantage. The families – many of them single-parent – represented what has now been accepted as Britain's underclass. There were many problem children in school, who manifested disruptive behaviour, and crime was prevalent. Educational standards were far below average.

This headteacher would generally take whole school assembly every day whilst we, the teachers, sat at the side of the hall next to our respective classes. Yet, despite his fine mind, expansive knowledge and excellent education, this man was one of the worst teachers I have ever encountered. He seemed to have absolutely no grasp at all of the level of understanding and sphere of interest of the children whom he addressed. He typically spoke to them of specific great composers, referring to the names of symphonies or operas, as if his audience were familiar with them. He read them sections – unabridged – of Shakespeare's plays, and consistently used vocabulary that would have challenged many university students. His apparently total lack of understanding of the minds and the home backgrounds of these children was amazing. Yet still – despite appalling behaviour on the part of the children – he persisted, day after day, along the same lines, never seeming to realize the extent of his incompetence as a teacher. Moreover, this ineptitude was not confined to assemblies: it was similarly displayed when – much to the horror of class teachers – he taught their classes when they were out of school. He was despised by almost all of the staff, and had no credibility as a headteacher. This was predominantly on account of his incapacity to do the very job in which he was employed to provide leadership. Indeed, when recalling this man I am amused by the applicability to him of one of a list of humorous excerpts taken from Royal Navy and Marines Fitness reports (Anon., 1997): 'His men would follow him anywhere, but only out of curiosity'.

Similarly, though none seems to have been as inept as this man with whom I once worked, headteachers who were considered by my interviewees to be poor teachers lost much respect:

Geoff hasn't much idea about the classroom side of it – you ask him for ideas on teaching and he's pretty clueless, really ... I mean, he just says, 'Oh, you're better at it than me – I wish *I* had so many ideas!' (Elaine, Rockville teacher)

If she [Mrs Hillman] goes into someone's class she doesn't *teach*, she just sits and goes through a box of files. ... And, I thought she was strict, but I was once watching a demonstration by a PE adviser in the hall – and I had the classroom next to the hall and you could see into it from the hall, through the windows – and she took my class ... and while I was in there, with the advisers and teachers from different schools, I could see my kids running around and jumping over chairs and all sorts of things ... and I thought she must have been back in her office ... but when I went in she was just sat at the desk, and she showed no interest in the education of the children and the activities that they were doing. (Mark, Leyburn teacher)

Assessments that determined headteachers' credibility as teachers were not confined to evaluation of their capacity to control children effectively and to teach imaginatively: they also included consideration of the extent and accuracy of their knowledge:

In a school this size ... you probably *would* justify a headteacher being ... non-teaching. But, I think, personally, I just feel he [Geoff] is so far removed from the practical realities of the classroom that you don't respect what he *does* do and what he might do ... well ... efficiently ... and, the meetings ... *personally* – I'm not talking about the rest of the school – but, *personally*, er ... I don't know what – he must attend a lot of meetings – but he doesn't carry a lot of weight because of the lack of direction that he manifests in the school. I'll give you an example ... he came in and said to me, 'How many first phase [ESL] children have you got, really?', and I said, 'Well, if I'm honest, only one ... the others were all born here'. I said, 'They've got limited English but their needs are different from this first phase child'. 'Really!', he said, 'I've never thought of that'. Well ... I mean ... to *me*, he's no perception of children's needs. ... It's the ... it's the sensitivity to psychological development and child development that he doesn't seem to ... understand, when applying ... er, his philosophies ... you know? To me, he just lacks a basic, fundamental understanding of child development. (Hilary, ESL teacher, employed at Rockville-based Language Centre)

But, she [Mrs Hillman] is not competent in the classroom. The most awful thing I've heard her say was ... very briefly – at one time she decided she'd have a little withdrawal group, and it was a special needs group – and she suddenly said, 'You know, I've been teaching all this time and I've suddenly realized that some of these naughty ones can be very nice!' And I was absolutely appalled. You see, it's always the nice children from good homes who get to play the brass instruments, and who do this and that ... and I once fought to get a child from the Commune into her other special needs group – the one for gifted children, and *I* thought this child was very clever ... couldn't spell – a hopeless speller – but very clever ... and she didn't

> want him in. He was a bit scruffy-looking, and he wasn't a conforming child … and to say, after twenty-odd years of teaching, 'I've just realized that some of these naughty children can be quite nice!' It's an *appalling* indictment, isn't it? – 'Can be very nice'! (Ann, Leyburn teacher)

> At South Street … the head knew nothing of what he was talking about so, I mean, although he had the ultimate responsibility, in actual fact he hadn't a lot of *power* … er … vested in him by the staff. (Amanda, Rockville teacher, speaking of a former headteacher)

On the other hand, headteachers who were considered to be effective teachers, with a sound understanding of pedagogy, were also those who were reported as the most effective leaders and motivators:

> Oh, he was very pedagogically aware! Oh, yes. He was Montessori trained … he'd done a Montessori course … oh, he could blind you with science! I mean, he's doing an M.Phil. now … oh, yes, he was very much more educationally aware than Mrs Hillman. … And he had some *super* ideas – he did some lovely things with the kids. … He was very well-read … and he cared very much about the children. (Ann, Leyburn teacher, speaking of a former headteacher)

> She was a full-time teaching head … a very well-organized person, and a very good classroom teacher … but, I learned a lot from her … the attention to detail in planning. If she did a topic it was well planned, and it was very thorough, and it was very good – she got some superb work from the kids … er … and I learned, from her, the attention to detail that I didn't *really* … that I'd never really bothered about so much. But, if she was going to do something, she did it well … whatever it was was done well. (Ann, Leyburn teacher, speaking of a former headteacher)

> And he [Phil] is very positive with the children. … On the whole, he likes to work through praise, and if the children are naughty he'll go through the disappointment bit first, rather than just say that they've been really naughty – and he tries to appeal to their better nature. … He's very good like that, and in assemblies I think he's very good with them. (Kay, Sefton Road teacher)

One of the best ways of raising your credibility amongst those whom you lead is to demonstrate your competence as a teacher. If you hold what is effectively a non-teaching role you should try to ensure that your teaching skills are displayed as publicly as possible on a number of occasions. You do not need to take on a regular teaching commitment in order to do so – most teachers appreciate the demands on headteachers' time, so it is with *how*, rather than *how often*, you teach that they will be most concerned. Colleagues will be particularly interested in how you manage children's behaviour, whether the activities that you provide are appropriate for the children and, to some extent, how well organized you are. It is important that your teaching competence is *seen*, so that word of it may spread amongst the staff. If you do not have opportunities to teach a class 'on view', such as in an open plan area, you will have to seize other opportunities that present themselves, such as leading assemblies. Nias *et al.* (1989, pp. 102-3), describing the 'collaborative' schools that they researched, refer to the positive effects on the headteacher–staff relationship that resulted from headteachers' enhancing their professional credibility through the use of school assemblies:

> Heads appear to set great store by leading through example . . . and all the heads of the project schools were aware of the power of example. Each head consciously expected to influence staff through his/her example . . . four of the five heads took assemblies:
>> . . . When the head told me she didn't take a class, I asked her if this had ever raised the question of her credibility. Her reply was that this must surely come through in her assemblies and in the way that she reacts to the children and deals with them. (Fieldnote, January, Lowmeadow)

You also need to make it clear that you know *about* teaching, understand what the work involves, and appreciate the problems that accompany it. Again, Nias *et al.* (1989, p. 104) illustrate how one headteacher managed to do this:

> But teaching did not always go smoothly. When the teaching was challenging, one head admitted to experiencing difficulty and 'exhaustion' and did not set unrealistic standards:
>> At the end of the afternoon Isobel staggers into the staffroom itself – parody. She has had the reception/middle class for the day and is shattered. I asked her if she would like a cup of tea and she says she'd rather I get the bottle out, which she proceeds to do. Part of the head–staff relationship at Sedgemoor is Isobel's openness. She makes no pretence of having found the class anything other than difficult. She says to everybody that comes in: 'You can't talk to them, they always want to tell you about themselves'. As staff arrive she tells them the story of what had happened during the day. . . . Here is the security of being able to allow others to laugh at you, and offering them the chance. You share your success and your disasters. (Fieldnote, February, Sedgemoor)

If you do not regularly teach – or have few opportunities to do so – you could convey your awareness and understanding of what the job involves through reference to some of the things that you did when you were a class or subject teacher, and through making helpful suggestions and offering useful ideas.

The essential point that you need to convey to colleagues is that you are capable of doing the job that they do. Research evidence of the importance of this is provided, once again, by Nias *et al.* (1989, pp. 104-5):

> For their part the teachers appreciated not only the heads' direct involvement in teaching but also their skills and effectiveness as practitioners. As one teacher said:
>> The fact is that everybody here probably knows that she can do your job as well as you and is quite happy to do it and not say 'I'm head now, I don't have to do that kind of thing any more. I'll just sit in my office and push the paperwork around'. (Teacher, Lavender Way)
> Clearly, these teachers perceived effective classroom practice as a prerequisite for leadership.

Whether you are a headteacher or principal, deputy head or assistant principal, head of a department or a teaching team, you do not have to demonstrate that you can do the job that other teachers do better than any of them, so a reputation as the best teacher in the school is unnecessary – although, of course, it would not do you any harm. As long as you convince most people that you have a reasonably high level of competence you will sustain sufficient credibility to allow your views, ideas and suggestions to be respected and, perhaps, sought. Without this credibility you will be unable to match Lortie's (1975, p. 197) image of a headteacher, which could just as easily be applied to any school leader:

> The principal as a symbol is ... important; as the 'instructional leader' of the school, he is an enhanced senior colleague. Thus he can symbolize professional purpose and competence: he potentially can reassure teachers about the quality of their teaching.

Credibility as an intellectual

I have already suggested in Chapter 3 that the school leader does not have to be the most 'extended' professional in the school or department. S/he does, however, need to be recognized as one of the most reflective, analytical and 'intelligent' members of staff. Applying once again the teacher–student parallel, consider how ridiculous would be a situation in which the children were generally more academically competent, more studious and more knowledgeable than their teacher. Yet, some of my interviewees expressed contempt for what they reported as their headteachers' manifestation of a lower intellectual capacity than that manifested by most of the staff:

> I don't think she [Mrs Hillman] is well-read. I think all her received wisdom's come from pamphlets and ... er ... stuff that you *have* to do. I

think that all the stuff that comes to her on the national curriculum she will
have *read*, but I don't think she's widely-read. (Ann, Leyburn teacher)

I just think . . . well, that the woman [Mrs Hillman] is lacking in intelligence
as well as anything else. . . .
   She's got no concept about theory. (Mark, Leyburn teacher)

But, what we're talking about now . . . I mean, my present head – he
wouldn't understand what we're on about. He wouldn't *disagree* with it – he
probably would think he was doing it. He just – I can't describe his . . . well,
he hasn't got a clue! . . . He's thick! He's one of the most unintelligent men
I know!
   . . . They're two male members of staff – the head and the deputy – and they
cannot see that that has implications for equal opportunities in the school!
They seem to think that, because we've got one girl who plays football,
that's it . . . and because the names on the registers are mixed they think
everything's working OK. (Helen, Woodleigh Lane teacher)

Clearly, as I have illustrated with the example earlier in this
chapter of one of the headteachers with whom I, as a teacher, once
worked, intellectual credibility alone is not enough to manage teachers effectively. However intelligent you appear to others, you will fail
to motivate them if you do not also manifest other essential school
leadership skills that determine your overall credibility. You must
not, though, be perceived as the 'dunce' on the staff. You must be
manifestly capable of conducting meaningful, intelligent discussions
with any of your colleagues, as well as with parents, governors and
visitors.

It is important to appreciate that qualifications do not necessarily
equate with – or accurately reflect – intellectual capacity. It is much
better to be able to impress others and give them confidence in your
ability by being able to present – and follow – a reasoned argument,
than to have MA or M.Ed. after your name. Of course, if you can offer
both, so much the better. In general, probably the single most
intelligent way of carrying out your school leadership role is to make
sure that your decisions always have a sound reason behind them,
that you can – and do – explain to your colleagues. Unintelligent
leadership features decision-making that is based on assumption and
prejudice and that is not well thought out – doing things because
they have always been done, without considering alternatives. Moreover, if a colleague presents an idea or a proposal to you, and if it is
well thought out and based on sound reasoning, no matter how
much you dislike it you should always accept it if you cannot present
a rational argument for rejecting it. The Teacher Training Agency
(TTA) in the UK includes in its list of national standards for headteachers reference to decision-making skills:

> Headteachers should be able to:
> i. make decisions based upon analysis, interpretation and understanding of relevant data and information;
> ii. think creatively and imaginatively to anticipate and solve problems and identify opportunities;
> iii. demonstrate good judgement. (TTA, 1998, p. 7)

Having intellectual credibility as a leader – whether you are a headteacher or principal or any other kind of school leader – requires the demonstration of these decision-making skills.

It is also important that you accept – and openly recognize – that you may have colleagues who are currently more capable than you, intellectually. (My use of the word 'currently' indicates my belief that anyone sufficiently motivated to do so will be able to increase his/her intellectual capacity.) You need to be seen to respect and utilize – not resent – what such colleagues have to offer to the school or department, and to your leadership of it. Making sure that you do not threaten your credibility by stepping over the line of what you may reasonably ask them to do without their feeling that they may as well be doing your job – and drawing your salary – you can take opportunities of enlisting the help of more 'gifted' colleagues in undertaking tasks that you find difficult:

> 'Amanda, I've just received this consultation paper from County Hall ... I know how good you are at picking up on details that I sometimes miss ... I wonder if you could spare the time to have a look at it, too, and we could compare notes next week.'

Most importantly, in the interests of maintaining openness and honesty, do not try to cover up your occasional reliance on others. You will win much more respect by acknowledging, not only that you have had the sense to recognize your own limitations (provided they are not too numerous) and to solicit help, but also that you are aware of others' strengths:

> 'I called this meeting to present this paper that I've prepared and get some idea of your views on it. I've already asked Abdul to have a look at what I've written, because, as we all know, he's very good at spotting flaws in arguments, and he was able to spot a couple that I'd made – which I've now rectified – so, thank you very much for that, Abdul.'

It is important to remember that, as a leader within a profession that now requires a first degree as a minimum entry requirement and that is generally considered to be represented by an intelligent, well-educated workforce, your credibility amongst your colleagues is dependent upon your carrying out your leadership role intelligently. Above all, what you must avoid is behaving in such a way that invites descriptors such as the final amusing item in the list of excerpts – to which I have referred earlier in this chapter – taken from Royal Navy and Marines Fitness reports (Anon., 1997): 'This man is depriving a village somewhere of an idiot'.

Credibility as a leading professional

If you hold a leadership position, quite simply you will be expected to lead. Your credibility with colleagues will be very reliant upon your knowing what your particular leadership role requires you to know, understanding what it requires you to understand, doing what it requires you to do, and achieving what it requires you to achieve. As I have illustrated in earlier chapters, though, not all of the head-teachers of whom my interviewees spoke manifested qualities and characteristics that might reasonably be expected of a leading professional.

In cases where 'extended' professionals were led by headteachers whose professionality was more 'restricted', these headteachers often lacked the professional credibility to be able to offer any kind of direction that would have been acceptable to many of their teacher colleagues. Geoff Collins, of Rockville, was such a head. Not only did his own reasoning lack depth and reflect limited insight, but he was unreceptive and impervious to the reasoned arguments of others. Geoff's headship lacked the 'leading professional' dimension, which Coulson (1988, p. 257) identifies as a potential source of conflict with a head's role as 'chief executive'.

Geoff did not appear to operate at a high level of abstraction, but merely at a lower level of day-to-day actions. This was recognized by all of the Rockville staff. He was never credited with superiority in relation to knowledge and understanding of educational issues, pedagogy, or curriculum development; indeed, Hilary, the ESL Language Centre teacher, described Geoff:

> He's inadequate because he's no sense of direction ... *he's* not directing the school – it's the tail that's wagging the dog! ... If the body of us was going in one direction he would go that way ... because he's powerless ... he is *not* a person who – he's in the wrong job – his personality's wrong for this kind of job ... especially in *this* kind of school. Er ... and, intellectually ... he doesn't worry about – nothing worries him! To me, he seems like the type who'll go home at night and go to sleep without a worry or a care ... there's no ... he's naïve, or oblivious, or insensitive, or *something* ... I don't know what the word is ... whereas ... it's just like it's passive – an abdication of responsibility ... Now, *I* may be wrong – he might be in there, working hard, but ... it's like ... Deborah makes the decisions ... he cannot decide on what day to have meetings, when he's free to choose a day – y'know? He has abdicated his responsibilities for decision-making. ... And I feel that I have no respect – I feel that if he was a strong, assertive manager, with his own ideas, and though I wouldn't agree with him, I would have respect ...

> d'you know what I mean? It's because he lacks depth in educational
> development – in the development that should be going on in the school
> – er ... his perceptions ... so that he's ... he's inadequate ... and you *feel*
> that you despise him for that, really – it sounds awful – but you *do* despise
> him, because he doesn't know what you're on about, really ... or, *I* know
> as much as he does.

Geoff's headship incorporated neither curriculum leadership nor
monitoring, which Webb and Vulliamy (1996) identify as aspects of
the role of primary headteachers in the UK, nor was he considered to
be a transformational leader (Southworth, 1994, p. 18). In a sense,
this probably occurred through an iterative process: Geoff did not
offer any real direction to his colleagues and, mainly on account of
his failure to do so, he was not respected as a headteacher. Yet,
because he was not respected professionally, had he bothered to
offer direction it would almost certainly have been disregarded or
circumvented by many of the staff. Another Rockville interviewee
highlighted what she perceived to be Geoff's limitations as a leading
professional:

> I think high morale comes from a school where ... the head is seen as a
> figure you can look up to and respect ... er ... he knows his pupils ...
> there's a good quality of leadership ... he's supportive of the staff and
> appreciative of the staff ... and not afraid to tell staff if they're not doing
> what they should be doing ... but Geoff would never, ever, do that.
> (Elaine)

In a similar way, the Leyburn head was not recognized as a leading
professional because of her prioritization of tasks that were not
considered to be leadership tasks, at the expense of those that
were:

> There's part of me that *respects* her a great deal ... because she *does* work
> hard ... but I think that a lot of her work is ... er ... meaningless ...
> mindless, needless work which could be delegated to somebody else ... I
> think she *makes* a lot of work and chases her own tail a lot of the time ... and
> a lot of – when I first went to Leyburn I thought, 'My goodness, this woman
> never stops!', but ... most of the time she is ... cleaning windows ...
> picking up litter ... sweeping up leaves. I mean, that's not what a head-
> mistress is paid to do! I think ... er ... some of her priorities are a little bit
> misplaced. (Ann, Leyburn teacher)

I am sure that everyone who reads this book will be acutely aware of
the need – in today's climate – for school leaders to keep abreast of
the changes that are taking place in the education system. If you are
a headteacher you will know that much of your job involves respond-
ing to change. This is certainly the picture in the UK, where the role
of the headteacher – and particularly the primary headteacher – has
undergone enormous change since the Education Reform Act was

implemented in 1988. Maintaining credibility as the leading professional in your school or department clearly involves being 'on the ball' and being fully aware of policy developments and changes that are planned for your sector of education, your subject, or your area of specialism.

In the UK the national standards for headteachers (TTA, 1998) reflect precisely the range and level of professional knowledge and understanding, skills and attributes that are required of a leading professional. Many of these are applicable to all school leaders – in the UK and abroad – who want to establish and maintain their credibility amongst colleagues. If you want to motivate through your own credibility, these standards provide an excellent yardstick against which to measure yourself.

Note

1 Section 11 teachers – funded by the UK government to provide additional dedicated ESL support.

CHAPTER 8

Managing to motivate:
The pay-back

Introduction

So far, we have looked at what school leaders need to do in order to motivate teaching staff. I have identified what teachers want from their leaders and how leaders, in turn, can give it. So the emphasis, throughout, has been very much on leaders' giving.

But why *should* school leaders give so much? What do *they* get out of managing to motivate? Is it actually worth the trouble? We all know of headteachers or heads of department who seem to pay very little attention to what their colleagues want. They do not appear to go out of their way to motivate staff, and yet they seem to run very efficient and effective schools or departments. So, is motivational leadership necessary?

In this final short chapter I examine managing to motivate from the perspective of what is in it for those who practise it – the motivators. I highlight some of the rewards that you can expect to reap if your staff management and leadership follow the guidelines that I have presented. In a sense, this chapter is intended to motivate *you* to motivate.

Reaping the rewards

As I have emphasized throughout this book, effective staff leadership in schools parallels effective class teaching. Unfortunately, though, just as it is sometimes difficult for teachers to know how successful they have been at 'reaching' children, because most children do not think to tell them, so, too, is it not always obvious to school leaders that they have motivated staff. How are they to know – unless they are explicitly told – whether they have enthused Miss Brown to spend more time than she would otherwise have spent on preparing her teaching resources, or whether the extra hour every evening that Mr Green spends mounting classroom displays is due to their having motivated him to do so, rather than his concern to avoid the rush-hour traffic?

Nevertheless, although much of your good work in motivating others may not always yield a recognizable pay-back that you can, with certainty, attribute to your efforts, you will be able to sense, in time, the benefits that you have accrued by taking the time and the trouble to get the best out of people. One secondary school headteacher to whom I have referred in Chapter 1 (Stephens, 1998b) clearly manages to pick up a sense of the success of his leadership – which is evidently close to the 'teacher-centred' approach that I advocate. He writes, for example: 'Be liberal in response to staff requests for absences – you will be rewarded many times over in most cases by appreciative staff putting in extra time in many other ways'. In particular, you may reasonably expect to be rewarded for your efforts in many different ways, which I outline below.

Lower staff turnover

Although, inevitably, staff will leave, turnover should be considerably decreased in a school or department where teachers enjoy their work and derive satisfaction from the sense of achievement that your recognition reinforces. Consider the examples that I have presented in earlier chapters of teachers who were desperate to change jobs because their headteachers failed explicitly to appreciate and recognize their efforts, achievement and potential. Yet, in contrast, if most of their individual job-related needs are being met, teachers will, predictably, be very reluctant to leave their posts. Indeed, only if other needs emerge that their current posts do not satisfy will they look for a change of job. These needs may be impossible for you to meet because you lack the necessary resources. Examples include: the need for promotion, or higher pay; the need for a job in a different part of the country, or even abroad; or the need for wider experiences, such as a different kind of pupil/student composition – a teacher may, for instance, want to gain experience of teaching in areas of social disadvantage because s/he has only ever taught in schools in affluent areas, or s/he may want experience of sixth form (16–18-year-olds) teaching because s/he has only ever taught in 11–16 schools. One of my Sefton Road teacher interviewees fell into this category. The extent of her satisfaction with her job is indicated by Kay's reluctance to leave Sefton Road, despite her ambitions to secure a deputy headship, which had prompted her to make several applications:

Interviewer. Now, do you enjoy it here?
Yes.
Interviewer. How much?
Well, it has its bad days ... I suppose everywhere does. Well, I mean, I'm applying for other jobs, but it isn't because I'm unhappy here ... and I feel that, because I'm happy, it gives me a position of strength when I'm looking for other jobs – I can be selective ... I'm not grabbing at straws, you know.
Interviewer. So, you obviously enjoy it here, Kay ... but it's not, in itself, a retainer?
It is in *some* respects because, even if I *was* offered another job, I would still consider it very carefully ... er ... because your peace of mind *is* important. ... If I was going to move to somewhere where I *was* unsettled, or where I did feel unhappy, then I just wouldn't go. I'd rather stay put.

Enhanced working atmosphere

You can expect very positive working relationships to develop from your 'teacher-centred' approach to school leadership, and these, in turn, will enhance your school's or department's professional culture and working atmosphere. Through managing to motivate you will foster what Nias *et al.* (1989) refer to as a 'culture of collaboration', and avoid the 'them-and-us' kind of atmosphere that reflects many schools' – and some departments' – leader–staff relations. In the context of my research, as my illustrations in earlier chapters indicate, the Leyburn culture was very much of the 'them-and-us' kind. The headteacher, Mrs Hillman, failed to motivate the staff and they resented her, personally, and her leadership:

> *Interviewer. Do you like her* [Mrs Hillman] *as a person?*
> [a second's hesitation] No ... not now.
> *Interviewer. Does she motivate you at all?*
> No.
> *Interviewer. Do you feel you're accountable to her? Do you do things because ... well, in another school, you'd perhaps slack off more?*
> Oh, yes, there is that. I think ... er ... well, no ... I *don't* do it – you see, there's a stubbornness in my nature. I *don't* change my wall displays regularly because she says 'Jump'.
> *Interviewer. Do you do things to please her?*
> No. (Ann, Leyburn teacher)

And when I've been on these courses, and they've offered models of leadership and management technique and communication ... and everybody slags off their head ... but, it's just *marginal* things with *them*. Here, it's just *everything* – the whole thing ... the school ... *everything* is wrong – but it looks alright from the outside. ... It's just a model of how *not* to be, as far as *I'm* concerned. (Mark, Leyburn teacher)

In contrast, when you manage to motivate teachers you will find your staff management role so much easier because colleagues will be on your side, working with, rather than against you. Quite simply, ask yourself if you would rather have *your* colleagues express about *you* the kind of sentiments that Ann and Mark expressed about Mrs Hillman, or the kind expressed by teachers who were motivated by their headteachers or principals:

> It was only a small school and so it was slightly different, and ... he would bring in Mars bars and say, 'I think we all deserve these' ... so, although there was the more flexible approach to time-keeping ... and sometimes he'd say, '*I'll* take the kids this morning – you get on with some work', and he'd keep them for a good hour, or so. But you worked every bit as hard for somebody like him ... every bit as hard ... and we were just all friends together ... I mean, we were just like one big happy family, really. (Ann, Leyburn teacher, speaking of a former head)

The heads were greatly respected, and were described by their staffs in warm and positive ways:

> *Interviewer. Can I ask you how you find Graham as a head?*
> Absolutely marvellous! I can't really say I've ever worked for a better head. I think as long as you're doing your job and getting on and giving of your best, I think Graham is quite happy. I think he knows what's going on but he's not heavy-handed, he just doesn't come round laying the law down. And he's very approachable, he's just fine. No problems with Graham. (Teacher, Greenfields)

... Indeed, so positive were these expressions of respect that it became clear that many of the staff had a strong affection, even love, for their head.

> She is always available, and if you feel that you needed to discuss something with her you could always ring her up and you know she'd be supportive, whenever. I think she's a friend rather than 'the leader'. I think that's important. (Teacher, Lavender Way)

> I think she's quietly supportive and that is a marvellous position to be in if you've got her support and she's there as an absolutely marvellous resource and I admire the way that she can help people without taking over ... we've all got to learn from her. (Teacher, Sedgemoor)

> Miss Proctor brings love, really. Caring with a capital C. (Teacher, Lowmeadow)
> (Nias *et al.*, 1989, pp. 109-10)

> The principal totally inspired us. We were never told to be positive; it was just catching. The principal was the key figure in the school. Even in Wonderland there were teachers who didn't like things about each other. I think a really effective principal can minimize problems in any situation, and turn teachers toward helping children. (Rosenholtz, 1991, p. 63)

As I have already suggested, with school leadership and management, over time, you generally reap what you sow. Although, sadly, you may not hear many of them, accolades such as these, reflecting teachers' appreciation of positive working atmospheres created by effective leadership, are what you can expect if you manage to motivate. The TTA's (1998, p. 5) observations about effective headship are equally applicable to effective school leadership at any level:

> Effective headship results in:
> a. schools where
>> i. there is a positive ethos, which reflects the school's commitment to high achievement, effective teaching and learning and good relationships ...

Teacher development

By leading your school or department in a way that allows those teachers who want it a part in the decision-making process, and that facilitates everyone's reaching her/his full potential, you will be enabling staff and encouraging their professional development. If you follow the guidelines that I present throughout this book you will be well on track to attain those of the national standards for head-teachers that the TTA (1998, p. 11) categorizes as relating to leading and managing staff – one of five of what it identifies as 'key areas of headship', but most of which, again, have wider school leadership applicability. In relation to teacher development the TTA observes that headteachers:

>> iv. motivate and enable all staff in their school to carry out their respective roles to the highest standard, through high quality continuing professional development based on assessment of needs;
>> v. lead professional development of staff through example; support and co-ordinate the provision of high quality professional development ...

Managing this – whatever level of school leadership you represent – constitutes an excellent contribution to teacher development and an impressive achievement on your part. There is clear evidence that school leaders are capable of having an impact on teacher develop-ment – indeed, I have included such evidence in earlier chapters. Chapter 1, for example, includes Helen's description of a former headteacher who, she believed, influenced her professional develop-ment. Helen also said of the same headteacher:

> She had a very strong educational vision. ... Now, up until that time – I mean, I'm a much slower learner – I was piecing together my educational philosophy and, a lot of the time, just ... you know, struggling to get by ... er ... and she really just turned me round like nobody else ever has done. ... She was very, very challenging on a direct level ... I mean, she insisted,

right from the start, that we do a planning book every week, and she had that in, first thing on a Monday morning – and, woe betide you if you had any lame excuse as to why the book wasn't there! And she would read those on a Monday morning, and have them back to you by playtime! ... with copious comments, and, 'Why don't you ... ?' and things like that. So she, kind of, developed ... er ... you know, what you were doing, and asked questions. ... And ... what she was focusing on, as it became apparent through all her notes that she was writing, was actually the children's experience – 'cos what most people write in a planning book is what they're going to *teach* ... which isn't the same thing at all. ... Er, so, in that way she challenged people. She then spent a lot of time *in* the classroom ... and, she'd remember what you'd put in your planning book, and so she came round to see it in practice, and asked you how it'd gone on.

Rozenholtz's study (1991, p. 89) revealed similar evidence:

> Well, I was having some difficulty last year. And everyone pitched in and helped me. My principal took lots of time with me, explaining things, and made sure I got a chance to talk to other teachers ... it wasn't so much with teaching materials, though everyone was really generous with those. It was more with teaching problems: how to handle children who didn't know their multiplication tables; how to involve this child or that child; what to do when kids didn't do their homework ...

This teacher describes a setting in which colleagues and principal unofficially work together to support growth and to provide in a communal way for new teachers. And here ... we find principals to be the indisputable linchpin in helping poorly performing teachers to improve. In fact, 85 per cent of the teachers from learning-enriched schools report constructive principal involvement with troubled teachers: through frequent and clear evaluation; their own suggestions and advice; and their mobilization of resources, particularly the school's teacher leaders. Through these actions principals communicate no small degree of certainty that ineffective teachers can be helped to improve.

Rosenholtz (1991, p. 90) refers, too, to principals who 'establish norms of continuous improvement'. She adds: 'Their tactics are not to ferret out and penalize ineffectiveness, but rather to devise ingenious ways of putting new information and experiences within the reach of ... teachers in order to improve the quality of their work'.

Improving the quality of teachers' work in your school or department is certainly a pay-back that is well worth having, and it is a pay-back that is within the grasp of 'teacher-centred' school leaders who present to their colleagues an image of personal and professional credibility.

A better school

The more their needs are met, the more satisfied people will be. Managing to motivate teachers sets off a cyclical chain reaction of positive outcomes: high levels of job satisfaction lead to high morale, and teachers – happy in their jobs – are motivated towards sustained, or even increased, effort and performance ... and so the cycle is perpetuated until something occurs to break the chain. From all this, though, comes overall higher quality performance – better teaching – than what would otherwise occur. And, at the end of all this, what you have is a better school or department. Tony Stephens (1998b) explains the link between school leadership that involves 'really caring for ... teachers' and better educational provision. Referring to the management tips that he lists, he suggests:

> If all the above were adopted nationwide it would be a greater contribution to raising the achievement levels in schools than anything else introduced in the last 10 years – the happier the teachers, the better taught the students and the better our schools.

Of course, there is a little bit of generalization and oversimplification involved in this equation. For example, there are some individuals – you may know of some, or you may be one yourself – who are sufficiently self-motivated to sustain an optimum level of performance, come what may. These people will always give of their best, however they are managed, and so a 'teacher-centred' approach to school leadership will secure from them nothing more – in relation to output – than any other leadership approach. Dissatisfaction with and frustration by management will not diminish their performance of their job – but they may prompt them to *give up* their job. We have seen the research evidence that this does occur, and if – as is often the case – these people are outstandingly good teachers then what you are left with is a worse, not a better, school or department.

I do not claim that 'teacher-centred' school leadership brings about improved teaching from everyone, all the time. There will always be one or two individuals – a very small minority – whom you may never 'reach', and those whom you do motivate will not necessarily achieve their full potential continually. But neither will you. Overall, though, you will reap the reward of getting the very best out of nearly everyone, for most of the time – which, when it translates into quality of educational provision, is quite a pay-back.

Job fulfilment

Finally, managing to motivate – and, through that, getting the best out of teachers so that, between you, you raise the quality of education that your school or department provides – all adds up to a significant achievement. When you begin to notice the impact of your 'teacher-centred' leadership approach you will feel that you have really achieved something valuable and worthwhile, and this will be enormously fulfilling for you. Although you may not receive frequent feedback on your leadership – probably because it will simply not occur to most people to offer feedback to their leaders, or perhaps because good leadership soon becomes taken for granted by those fortunate enough to experience it – on the occasions when you do, and when the feedback is very positive, it will give you a real lift. You may very well have experienced this already if you have thought-ful, appreciative colleagues.

The potential for job fulfilment of effective staff management and leadership is enormous, and you become aware of this fact once you stop to consider the full range of achievements that could emanate from it, such as:

- being directly responsible for influencing people's prac-tice – for the better;
- successfully mentoring and preparing someone for pro-motion;
- raising someone's self-confidence and self-esteem;
- encouraging colleagues' reflectivity – and seeing develop-ment occur;
- introducing a more democratic system of decision-making – and seeing it work;
- reducing dissatisfaction amongst staff;
- watching colleagues who, when you first took up your post, were fed up and were applying for other jobs, change their minds;

and many, many more. The job fulfilment potential of effective school leadership is reflected in one primary headteacher's response to researchers' questions about her enjoyment of the job:

> I absolutely enjoy it, but I do say that if you feel you have wonderful people to share the job with, then it is manageable . . . if you do have lovely teachers and governors and children to share it, every single day is different and that is wonderful. (Pascal and Ribbins, 1998, p. 147)

Appendix

Outline of research design

The research findings that form the basis of this book emerged out of a composite study of morale and job satisfaction amongst primary school teachers in the UK. This comprised four studies, carried out from 1988 to 1992, each having a different focus within the broad overall remit of identifying and examining factors which influence teacher morale and job satisfaction. Study 1 was a pilot study of morale in a single primary school and involved a sample of thirteen teachers. In addition, to gain a 'non-teacher' perspective, I interviewed the secretary of the pilot school. Study 2 investigated further what had emerged from the pilot study as a very significant finding: the degree of match between teachers' professionality orientations (see Chapter 3) and the professionality, first, shown by their head-teachers and, second, reflected in their schools' prevailing professional climates. This involved the pilot study school and two other primary schools, and a total sample of nineteen teachers. In the cases of the thirteen Rockville [the pilot study school] teachers, though, I did not re-interview them for this study. Their involvement in it was confined to my re-analysis of the data provided by their pilot study interviews. Study 3 focused exclusively on the morale and job satisfaction, and other job-related attitudes, of teachers who could be categorized as 'extended' professionals, and involved six teacher case studies. Five of these case study teachers had participated in Studies 1 or 2. Study 4 was carried out in 1992 and was a post-Education Reform Act (of 1988) follow-up of the initial pilot study, using a sample of eight of the thirteen pilot study teachers. Its purpose was to ascertain whether or not, and to what extent, centrally-initiated factors such as the implementation of the national curriculum and the testing procedures which accompanied it had displaced the prominence of school-specific issues and circumstances as morale- and job satisfaction-influencing factors.

Data collection was predominantly qualitative. For Studies 1 and 2 I employed a form of participant observation, involving my adopting a role of part-time support teacher–observer over several months, which gave me valuable insight into contextual circumstances and a background knowledge of everyday life in the sample schools. I also used semi-structured interviews with teachers in all four studies, and self-completion post-interview questionnaires in Study 1 were used as a means both of quantifying individuals' levels of morale and job satisfaction, and of ascertaining the width of applicability of interview-generated data. (Further details of the research design, including core interview questions, methods of data analysis, and measures adopted to maximize construct validity, are provided in Evans, 1998.) The four studies and details of the sample used are summarized in Tables 1 and 2.

Table 1   Outline details of the research design of the composite study

| Study | Focus of enquiry | Dates | Sample | | Method(s) of data collection |
			No. of schools	No. of teachers	
(i) Rockville	Investigation of the morale level at Rockville County Primary School and of the factors influencing it	1988-89	1	13	(i) Observation (ii) Semi-structured interview (iii) Questionnaire
(ii) school climate	Investigation of the effects on teachers' attitudes to their jobs of the combination of school climate and teachers' professionality	1989-90	3	19	(i) Observation (ii) Semi-structured interview
(iii) 'extended' professionality case studies	Investigation of factors affecting the job-related attitudes of 'extended' professionals	1990-92	4	6	Semi-structured interview
(iv) post-ERA follow-up	Investigation of the comparative effects on teachers' attitudes to their jobs of school-specific and centrally-imposed factors	1992-93	1	8	Semi-structured interview

Table 2 Details of the teacher sample involved in the composite study

Pseudonym	Age at time of first interview	No. of times interviewed	Job status	School	Studies in which involved *(as numbered in Table 1)*
Elaine	35	1	Mainscale	Rockville	(i), (ii)
Rosemary	52	2	(i) A allowance-holder (ii) Deputy head	Rockville	(i), (ii), (iii), (iv)
Brenda	39	2	Mainscale	Rockville	(i), (ii), (iv)
Stephen	33	1	Mainscale	Rockville	(i), (ii)
Barbara	25	2	Mainscale	Rockville	(i), (ii), (iv)
Jane	40	2	Mainscale	Rockville	(i), (ii), (iv)
Pat	41	2	Mainscale	Rockville	(i), (ii), (iv)
Joanne	49	1	Mainscale	Rockville	(i), (ii)
Susan	30	2	Mainscale	Rockville	(i), (ii), (iii), (iv)
Jean	55	2	Mainscale	Rockville	(i), (ii), (iv)
Amanda	45	2	Mainscale	Rockville	(i), (ii), (iii), (iv)
Lesley	31	1	Mainscale	Rockville	(i), (ii)
Hilary	36	1	ESL mainscale	Rockville	(i), (ii)
Deborah	43	1	School secretary	Rockville	(i)
Helen	42	2	(i) B allowance-holder (ii) C allowance-holder	(i) Woodleigh Lane (ii) Ethersall Grange	(iii)
Kay	42	1	B allowance-holder	Sefton Road	(ii), (iii)
Sarah	28	1	Mainscale	Sefton Road	(ii)
Louise	40	1	Mainscale	Sefton Road	(ii)
Mark	32	1	Mainscale	Leyburn	(ii), (iii)
Fiona	41	1	Mainscale	Leyburn	(ii)
Ann	42	1	Mainscale	Leyburn	(ii)

References

Andain, I. (1990) Protest of the undervalued, *Guardian*, 17 April.

Anon. (1991) Which comes first, money or quality?, *The Times Educational Supplement*, 8 February, p. 23.

Anon. (1997) Bottom line, *Guardian*, 6 February, p. 15.

Baehr, M.E. and Renck, R. (1959) The definition and measurement of employee morale, *Administrative Science Quarterly*, 3, pp. 157-84.

Ball, S.J. (1987) *The Micro-Politics of the School*, London, Routledge.

Belasco, J. and Alutto, J. (1975) Decisional participation and teacher satisfaction. In V. Houghton, R. McHugh and C. Morgan (eds), *Management in Education: the Management of Organisations and Individuals*, London, Ward Lock Educational in association with Open University Press.

Blackbourne, L. (1990) All's fair in the hunt for better jobs, *The Times Educational Supplement*, 11 May, p. A4.

Brighouse, T. and Woods, D. (1999) *How to Improve your School*, London, Routledge.

CACE (The Plowden Report) (1967) *Children and their Primary Schools*, Vol. 1, London, HMSO.

Chandler, B.J. (1959) Salary policies and teacher morale, *Educational Administration and Supervision*, Vol. 45, pp. 107-10.

Chapman, D.W. (1983) Career satisfaction of teachers, *Educational Research Quarterly*, 7(3), pp. 40-50.

Chase, F.S. (1953) Professional leadership and teacher morale, *Administrator's Notebook*, Vol. 1, No. 8, pp. 1-4.

Coughlan, R.J. (1970) Dimensions of teacher morale, *American Educational Research Journal*, 7, pp. 221-34.

Coulson, A.A. (1988) An approach to headship development through personal and professional growth. In M. Clarkson (ed.), *Emerging Issues in Primary Education*, Lewes, Falmer.

Day, C., Hall, C. and Whitaker, P. (1998) *Developing Leadership in Primary Schools*, London, Paul Chapman.

Department for Education and Employment (DfEE) (1998) *Teachers Meeting the Challenge of Change*, London, DfEE.

Elliott, J. (1991) A model of professionalism and its implications for teacher education, *British Educational Research Journal*, Vol. 17, No. 4, pp. 309-18.

Evans, L. (1992) Teacher morale: an individual perspective, *Educational Studies*, Vol. 18, No. 2, pp. 161-71.

Evans, L. (1997a) Understanding teacher morale and job satisfaction, *Teaching and Teacher Education : an international journal of research and study*, Vol. 13, No. 8, pp. 831-45.

Evans, L. (1997b) Leading from the front, *Guardian Education*, 11 February, p. 6.

Evans, L. (1997c) Managing to motivate: some pointers for primary headteachers, *Primary School Manager*, July/August, pp. 16-18.

Evans, L. (1998) *Teacher Morale, Job Satisfaction and Motivation*, London, Paul Chapman.

Evans, L., Packwood, A., Neill, S. and Campbell, R.J. (1994) *The Meaning of Infant Teachers' Work*, London, Routledge.

Farrugia, C. (1986) Career-choice and sources of occupational satisfaction and frustration among teachers in Malta, *Comparative Education*, 22(3), pp. 221-31.

Galloway, D., Boswell, K., Panckhurst, F., Boswell, C. and Green, K. (1985) Sources of satisfaction and dissatisfaction for New Zealand primary school teachers, *Educational Research*, 27(1), pp. 44-92.

Goodson, I.F. (1991) Sponsoring the teacher's voice: teachers' lives and teacher development, *Cambridge Journal of Education*, 21, pp. 35-45.

Guba, E.G. (1958) Morale and satisfaction: a study in past–future time perspective, *Administrative Science Quarterly*, 3, pp. 195-209.

Guion, R.M. (1958) Industrial morale: the problem of terminology, *Personnel Psychology*, 11, pp. 59-64.

Halpin, A.W. (1966) *Theory and Research in Administration*, New York, Macmillan.

Hayes, D. (1996) Taking Nothing for Granted, *Educational Management and Administration*, 24(3), pp. 291-300.

Hayes, L.F. and Ross, D.D. (1989) Trust versus control: the impact of school leadership on teacher reflection, *Qualitative Studies in Education*, Vol. 2, No. 4, pp. 335-50.

Herzberg, F. (1968) *Work and the Nature of Man*, London: Staples Press.

Hoppock, R. (1977) *Job Satisfaction*, New York, Arno Press.

Hoyle, E. (1975), Professionality, professionalism and control in teaching. In V. Houghton, R. McHugh and C. Morgan (eds), *Management in Education: the Management of Organisations and*

Individuals, London, Ward Lock Educational in association with Open University Press.

ILEA (1986) *The Junior School Project*, London, ILEA Research and Statistics Branch.

Johnson, S.M. (1986) Incentives for teachers: what motivates, what matters, *Educational Administration Quarterly*, Vol. 22, No. 3, pp. 54-79.

Kasten, K.L. (1984) The efficacy of institutionally dispensed rewards in elementary school teaching, *Journal of Research and Development in Education*, Vol. 17, No. 4, pp. 1-13.

Lawler, E.E. (1994) *Motivation in Work Organizations*, Monterey, CA: Brooks/Cole.

Locke, E. (1969) What is job satisfaction?, *Organizational Behavior and Human Performance*, 4, pp. 309-36.

Lortie, D.C. (1975) *Schoolteacher: A Sociological Study*, Chicago, University of Chicago Press.

Maslow, A.H. (1954) *Motivation and Personality*, New York, Harper and Row.

Mathis, C. (1959) The relationship between salary policies and teacher morale, *Journal of Educational Psychology*, Vol. 50, No. 6, pp. 275-9.

Mayston, D. (1992) *School Performance Indicators and Performance-Related Pay*, London, The Assistant Masters and Mistresses Association.

McAvoy, D. (1996) Forget the big stick, let teachers think for themselves, *Guardian Education*, 13 February, p. 5.

McLaughlin, M.W., Pfeifer, R.S., Swanson-Owens, D. and Yee, S. (1986) Why teachers won't teach, *Phi Delta Kappan*, February, pp. 420-6.

Mercer, D. and Evans, B. (1991) Professional myopia: job satisfaction and the management of teachers, *School Organisation*, Vol. 11, No. 3, pp. 291-301.

Mumford, E. (1972) *Job Satisfaction: A Study of Computer Specialists*, London, Longman.

Nias, J. (1980) Leadership styles and job satisfaction in primary schools. In Bush, T., Glatter, R., Goodey, J. and Riches, C. (eds), *Approaches to School Management*, London, Harper and Row, pp. 255-73.

Nias, J. (1981) Teacher satisfaction and dissatisfaction: Herzberg's 'Two-Factor' hypothesis revisited, *British Journal of Sociology of Education*, 2(3), pp. 235-46.

Nias, J. (1989) *Primary Teachers Talking: A Study of Teaching as Work*, London, Routledge.

Nias, J., Southworth, G. and Yeomans, R. (1989) *Staff Relationships in the Primary School: a Study of Organisational Cultures,* London, Cassell.

Pascal, C. and Ribbins, P. (1998) *Understanding Primary Headteachers,* London, Cassell.

Redefer, F.L. (1959) Factors that affect teacher morale, *The Nation's Schools,* 63(2), pp. 59-62.

Rosenholtz, S. (1991) *Teachers' Workplace: The Social Organization of Schools,* New York, Teachers College Press.

Schaffer, R.H. (1953) Job satisfaction as related to need satisfaction in work, *Psychological Monographs: General and Applied,* 67(14), pp. 1-29.

Sergiovanni, T.J. (1968) New evidence on teacher morale: a proposal for staff differentiation, *North Central Association Quarterly,* 42, pp. 259-66.

Smith, K.R. (1976) Morale: a refinement of Stogdill's model, *Journal of Education Administration,* 14(1), pp. 87-93.

Smith, K.R. (c.1988) *The structure of morale in organisations,* unpublished transcript provided by the author.

Southworth, G. (1994) School leadership and school development: reflections from research. In G. Southworth (ed.) *Readings in Primary School Development,* London, Falmer.

Steers, R.M., Porter, L.W. and Bigley, G.A. (1996) (6th edition) *Motivation and Leadership at Work,* New York, McGraw-Hill.

Stephens, T. (1998a) *366 Pieces of Advice for the Secondary Headteacher* (typescript booklet), Mill Hill School, Peasehill, Derbyshire DE5 3JG.

Stephens, T. (1998b) It all sounds obvious, but ... , *Guardian Education,* 15 December, p. 33.

Sutcliffe, J. (1997) Enter the feel-bad factor, *The Times Educational Supplement,* 10 January, p. 1.

Talbert, J.E. and McLaughlin, M.W. (1996) Teacher professionalism in local school contexts'. In I. Goodson and A. Hargreaves (eds) *Teachers' Professional Lives,* London, Falmer, pp. 127-53.

Teacher Training Agency (1998) *National Standards for Headteachers,* London, Teacher Training Agency.

Tomlinson, H. (1990) Performance rights?, *The Times Educational Supplement,* 9 November, p. 11.

Veal, M.L., Clift, R. and Holland, P. (1989) School contexts that encourage reflection: teacher perceptions, *International Journal of Qualitative Studies in Education,* Vol. 2, No. 4, pp. 315-33.

Vroom, V.H. (1964) *Work and Motivation,* New York, John Wiley and Sons.

Wallace, M. and Huckman, L. (1996) Senior management teams in large primary schools: a headteacher's solution to the complexities of post-reform management?, *School Organisation*, 16(3), pp. 309-23.

Webb, R. and Vulliamy, G. (1996) The changing role of the primary-school headteacher, *Educational Management and Administration*, 24(3), pp. 301-15.

Williams, G. (1986) *Improving School Morale*, Sheffield City Polytechnic, PAVIC Publications.

Williams, K.W. and Lane, T.J. (1975) Construct validation of a staff morale questionnaire, *Journal of Educational Administration*, 13(2), pp. 90-7.

Winston, J. (1992) The school management plan: a case study in the ethics of school management, *Journal of Teacher Development*, Vol. 1, No. 3, pp. 141-8.

Wortman, R. (1995) *Administrators Supporting School Change*, York, Stenhouse; Los Angeles, The Galef Institute.

Young, I.P. and Davis, B. (1983). The applicability of Herzberg's Dual Factor Theory(ies) for public school superintendants, *Journal of Research and Development in Education*, 16(4).

Index